SLAVERY NOW – AND THEN

An investigation into modern slavery
by leading human rights authorities of our time
in the context of the transatlantic slave trade

D1392322

Slavery Now – and Then

DANNY SMITH

KINGSWAY PUBLICATIONS
EASTBOURNE

Front cover photo by Hazel Thompson, used by permission.
Design for cover by Pinnacle Creative, UK.

ISBN 978 1 84291 331 4

KINGSWAY COMMUNICATIONS LTD
Lottbridge Drove, Eastbourne BN23 6NT, England.
Email: books@kingsway.co.uk

Printed in the USA

Contents

Foreword

Reverend Joel Edwards, General Director,
Evangelical Alliance

Geographical locations can often evoke the most poignant of emotions. As a Black British Christian whose ancestors were uprooted from Africa eight generations ago, retracing the path of the Zambian slave trail was as moving an experience as walking through Emancipation Park in Kingston, Jamaica, or standing on the spot where Martin Luther King was shot.

The year 2007 is another location. A chronological place reminding us of 200 years since the abolition of the slave trade in our nation, and carrying similar potential to stir within us many mixed emotions. On the one hand, there is celebration that no corner of civic society will not now voice its disgust at the very idea of slavery. And yet, on the other hand, there is despair that two centuries after the outlawing of the trade, slavery still exists in many parts of our world. In some it is even in the ascendancy. In an age when the concepts of liberty and anti-slavery have grown up together, modern-day slavery has managed to defy one and mock the other. A global glut of human suffering still stands to arrest our claims of universal progress and civilisation.

In the eighteenth- and nineteenth-century debates, slavery was sustained by a kind of ideological ambivalence, underwritten by pre-Enlightenment ideas. The unpleasant reality is that Christian teaching – not just Christianity as an institution – at its worst legitimised it and at its best did little more than subvert rather than repudiate it outright. In the genteel theological discussions, the exchange of ideas led eminent church leaders to interpret this ambivalence to mean that even Christian conversion did nothing to make the black man any more than the property of his European master. The drive for abolition was a battle to overcome these biblical ambiguities and political reticence: the black man's response was to insist that he was a Man and a Brother.

But as Eric Williams's study *Capitalism and Slavery* demonstrated, abolition was not only a matter of white benevolence, it was also a matter of economics. Slavery, Williams argued, was becoming a financial liability. Both then and now the travesty of human slavery has been to reduce human beings to profit. Black people were sardined into confined spaces not simply because slave traders were wicked, but because people were seen as 'things'. Perniciously, the cruelty of the slave trader was not in his brute force per se, but in the fact that his brutality was motivated by a desire to maximise profit. And then, as now, millions of men, women, boys and girls had their humanity obliterated, their bodies imprisoned and their spirits crushed in the name of greed.

In addition to ideological ambiguity and greed, slavery was fed by cultural superiority. Both the ostentation of the Caribbean plantation masters and the opulence of the East India Dock owners were a testament to cultural pride – cultural imperialism had to have something to show for itself. The inherent superiority complex of the European slave owner was reinforced by the sense of a cultural class system which subjugated the African way of life, raping it of identity, language and land.

What is frightening is that this triad of abuse – ideological ambivalence, profits from people and cultural superiority – is part of the deeply motivating factors behind slavery today. Slavery has always been much more complex than a simple issue of Black against White. People in all ages and of all cultures have been enslaved. The glories of Babylon, the Great Wall of China, the pyramids of Egypt and the City of London were all built on these values. Sadly, despite our celebrations of the anniversary of abolition, human greed and evil still exist and continue to sustain the monster that is human trafficking.

Fallen people have always been the same: barbarism is a by-product of our mangled humanity. A Christian response to human trafficking begins, therefore, not with the politics of trafficking, but with the reality of our sinfulness and greed which feed from and contribute to the sacrilege of human slavery. So prayer and spiritual militancy will be integral to the Christian response. But equally Christians must rise up from prayer to become fully global citizens. In the fight against slavery our distinct contribution must be added to that of the wider human family struggling to free the world of the scourge of human selling. In the year 2007 we have seen and said enough. No argument or economic circumstance can ever justify the terrible atrocity of slavery. This has always been the case, both now and then. But now we are without excuse.

REVEREND JOEL EDWARDS
Reverend Joel Edwards's appointment as General Director of the Evangelical Alliance UK was a historic event, as he became the first black Director in the Alliance's 150-year history. He was born in Jamaica and came to Britain at the age of eight. He is married to Carol and has two grown-up children. He was a probation officer for ten years and has drawn on his experience as a professional counsellor in a range of community-focused activities. He has been a member of the Home Office's Faith and Government Consultation Steering Group and the Home Secretary's National Policing Forum, and is working with the authorities to orchestrate a church response to the growing concerns over guns, gangs and violence in the UK. He is an accomplished broadcaster, appearing on BBC TV's *Question*

Time, BBC Radio 4's *Moral Maze* and *Any Questions* and Terry Wogan's *Pause for Thought* on BBC Radio 2.

For further information on Joel Edwards and the work of the Evangelical Alliance, see www.eauk.org.

Acknowledgements

Thanks to each of the contributors who immediately embraced the vision and supported the project with time and enthusiasm. Mike Morris reviewed the material and made important suggestions that enhanced and improved things significantly. Becky Tinsley played a critical part with zeal and speed. Luke Smith provided a critical eye for detail and constructive enthusiasm.

I am so grateful to Hazel Thompson for giving us permission to use her stunning photograph from her award winning portfolio 'Innocents Delivered', a series that was highly commended in the *Sunday Times* magazine's Ian Parry Award 2003.

Thanks also to others who worked behind the scenes: Barbara Mace, Bill Hampson, Rosemary Morris, Ben Rogers, Malcolm du Plessis, Karen Bishop, Vikki McLachlan, Mrs K. Lajja, Bex Keer at Stop the Traffik. And thanks, of course, to John Pac, Les Moir and Carolyn Owen at Kingsway who invited me to take up the venture.

This was completed at a time when relationships took on renewed meaning. I can never forget friends who stood with me through unprecedented turbulence and to whom I will remain always grateful: David Alton, Ann Buwalda, Father Shay Cullen, Dirk Jan Groot, John and Patsy Graham, Dr Kim and Sally Tan, James Parry, Olivia Harrison, Aninha Capaldi, Steve Brown, Andrew Smith, Alex Hermoso, Emma Foa and Reg Wright, Lois Brown, George Verwer, Sam Yeghnazar, Revd K. K. Deveraj, Shoba and Sandesh Kaddam, Hazel Thompson, 'Mike' from Homeland Security, Dr Wai Sin Hu, Roley Horowitz, Wanno Hanoveld, Frank and Marlene Rice, Paul Diamond, Eric Delve, John Smith, John Quanrad, David Muir, Bonnie Ryason, Ian and Rosemary Matthews, Sue Tatum, Ron George, Michele Lombardo, Mina Bahgat, Jim and Kitty Thompson. And finally to Mum, Clement and Joan, Jessica, Rachel and Luke – your love sustains me and is the most precious accompaniment on this journey.

Danny Smith

Introduction: Rescue the children

Danny Smith, Founder, Jubilee Campaign, Jubilee Action

The year 2007 is not the bicentenary of Britain's abolition of slavery. It is the date, 200 years ago, when parliament voted to end the shipping trade that transported enslaved Africans into the institution of slavery around the world.

About a million Africans remained enslaved for 30 years after 1807. As late as 1860, an American slave ship was seen picking up supplies in Liverpool, the city that had become the world capital of the slave trade, after capturing 60 per cent of England's deals and 40 per cent of the global business of slavery.

Nonetheless, 2007 is still an important date to mark because it represents a turning point – although the end of Britain's legalised enslavement of Africans came in 1838. Yet that was not to be the final word on the enslavement of people on our planet. Slavery was dealt a blow, but it recovered well.

Children in slavery

I first became aware of modern slavery in the early 1980s when I read an article by John Pilger in the *Daily Mirror*. The veteran investigative journalist reported how children were enslaved in prostitution in Thailand and revealed that he had literally bought a child – as undoubtedly others had. I carried the article with me and ordered all the photographs from the story, which included a bill of sale confirming the purchase. I always wanted to 'do something' on this issue, but the problem seemed too big. Our organisation – Jubilee Campaign, a human rights pressure group – was too small. Nothing we could do would make any difference. What was the point of doing anything?

All that changed the day I met Father Shay Cullen, an Irish priest in the Philippines, from the Columban missionary order.

While attending a mission conference in the Philippines in 1992, I dropped out of some sessions to talk to local agencies concerned about the problem of the commercial sex industry. Even a cursory glance confirmed that children were ensnared and enslaved. While most groups and churches I talked to had projects and an outreach programme, everyone directed me to an 'Irish priest' as the leading authority on the issue.

Father Shay patrolled the jails and the back streets of Olongapo City, once called the biggest brothel in the world. This was his parish. The street children and child prostitutes were his flock. His objective was to defend the rights of children and prosecute the offenders. He tracked down suspected paedophiles with the combined dedication of an Old Testament prophet and a modern-day detective.

Father Shay was practical and down to earth. He had none of the phony piousness of some church leaders, but displayed all the practical spirituality of someone who knew what it was like to live in the city. He had witnessed great evil and was compelled to confront it, within the context of his faith and experience. Father Shay explained his life's work in this way: 'I have a special mission to work for justice and peace and to bear witness to the truth. Part of my work is prophetic; that is, to take a stand for justice. Christianity in action is solidarity with very poor people, with those who have been oppressed, like in Olongapo, taking a stand, and not being intimidated but following in the footsteps of Jesus.

I'm not a moral crusader. I am fighting for justice. Justice is at the very heart of the message of Jesus. Working for justice is central to Christianity. Wherever justice is being done it is a sign that we love one another. I feel a righteous anger when I see injustice in the world – especially in the developing world and in countries like the Philippines – where the rich grow richer on the sweat of the poor.'

The fight begins

Father Shay and I became friends and partners and he showed me that we could have a role to play to help children trapped in sex slavery. Together we designed a campaign to fight child prostitution and launched this at a meeting in parliament in 1992, hosted by David Alton and the All Party Parliamentary Group on Street Children. David had helped us to set up the APPGSC and Jubilee Campaign served as its secretariat.

With MPs and the media in attendance at the meeting in the House of Commons, our campaign set out our objectives in a report that received wide coverage. It was important to demonstrate that as individuals, our anger and energy could have a practical expression to combat the structures of evil that were in place.

First, we wanted child prostitution declared a crime against humanity, similar to war crimes, with no statute of limitation. Second, we wanted courts in the UK to prosecute sex tourists.

No foreign government or Western nation had ever arrested any of its citizens who had abused children overseas and there was simply no mechanism in place to prosecute such offenders. At the time, Europeans could travel abroad and abuse children in places such as the Philippines with impunity; they could even videotape the abuse. If they were caught on foreign soil, the penalties were minimal and most could wriggle out of the charge with a fine or bribe to continue their abuse elsewhere. When they returned home, their secret was safe. If they were caught in Britain with the tape showing their abuse, they could be arrested for possessing obscene material on video – but not for the actual abuse. It was absurd. Meanwhile, large numbers of children were trapped in slavery and forced to endure the abuse.

At the parliamentary meeting, Father Shay provided the historical context from which to view this crime. His comments combined eloquence with clarity: 'Sex tourism and child prostitution is the ultimate in exploitation. Peoples of other nations have exploited the raw materials of poorer countries for centuries. Now they're coming back to exploit the bodies of our children.'

The statistics in our report proved sobering for everyone at the meeting in the House of Commons.

- Every year, about one million children were lured or forced into prostitution. This figure was documented in a Norwegian government report, confirming that young children were held as bait for a thriving attraction: sex with children.
- Globally, as many as ten million children were thought to be enslaved in the sex industry, prostitution and pornography.
- Child prostitution tended to be higher in Asia and Latin America, although an alarming growth rate had been recorded in Africa, North America and Europe. Eastern Europe and the former Communist states had emerged as a new market in the sexual exploitation of children.
- The UN Rapporteur on Child Trafficking had remarked recently that the children being tricked into prostitution were getting younger and younger. 'These are nine- ten- eleven- twelve-year-old kids,' he declared.

The experts were warning that the trend would increase unless action was taken.

Our campaign emphasised that the authorities that should have brought offenders to justice had failed, and they had used the system to evade capture, thus putting more children at risk.

It was time to cry, 'Enough!' Action was needed. The law must be changed to allow extraterritorial jurisdiction.

A brick wall

The government's response was not encouraging and the Home Office could not help. At a meeting led by MPs of the APPGSC, they told us that it was too difficult and complex a problem to change the law. It would never happen. Their logic was that such laws would be unworkable in practice because of the difficulties they perceived in gathering sufficient evidence from foreign jurisdictions to facilitate a successful prosecution in the UK. This argument was advanced despite the fact that similar laws existed for offences such as murder, suggesting that they would accept evidence for this criminal act, but not for crimes against children.

The Home Office insisted that it was not for the British government to impose its laws abroad. That was that.

To strengthen our efforts, we joined ECPAT (End Child Prostitution and Asian Tourism) but also continued several independent initiatives on the issue.

In 1994 our parliamentary officer, Wilfred Wong, a trained barrister-at-law, drafted a parliamentary bill setting out in detail the laws we sought.

Wilfred put a requirement of double criminality in the bill. This means that the alleged child sex offence had to be considered as a criminal offence both in the foreign country where it occurred and within the UK before the accused could be charged and prosecuted in this country.

He explained, 'I did this because I knew there was no way the British government would agree to imposing its laws on another jurisdiction if the crime in question was not even considered an offence in that foreign jurisdiction. Furthermore, I put in the requirement that nothing in the bill would contravene the legal principle of double jeopardy. This means that if the defendant had already been prosecuted and either convicted or acquitted for the offence while abroad, he could not be prosecuted for the same offence again when he returned to Britain.'

When Father Shay called from Olongapo and told me that an

Australian tourist had been arrested after police – at Father Shay's insistence – had caught him with three young children, one just seven years old, on board his yacht, I knew that the story was important. Shay had videotaped the dramatic arrest, and after seeing the footage I thought it would create a sensation if the media in Britain broadcast the pictures.

I hawked the tape around all the media offices and everyone who saw the raw footage was impressed and realised its potential. But when they heard that the abuser was Australian and not British, the story hit a brick wall. No one would run it.

Uncovering the truth

I knew that the best way to catch the politicians' eye and influence their opinion was to get the story into the media and onto the front page of the newspapers. With that strategic objective, I accepted a written invitation from *ITV News* to work with them on an undercover investigation into travel agents operating in Britain selling overseas child sex tours.

It was like a movie. The television crew took me to a car park, stripped me down and taped a small recording device and a secret camera to my body. The hidden camera tucked away out of sight under my clothes was attached to a miniature camera lens, virtually invisible, woven into an intricate design on a tie that I was given to wear. We were following a lead about a travel agent who operated near Chessington's World of Adventures selling child sex tours abroad, and I went undercover to 'enquire' about exactly what was on offer. The operation went well and in time we secretly recorded interviews with others in Britain who were involved in similar activities. It was horrifying to be talking to such people, but equally horrifying to know that their actions were not illegal.

The investigation with *ITV News* lasted several months and exposed disturbing evidence of people who exploited enslaved children and women overseas. I also worked closely with a journalist from Britain's biggest-selling newspaper, the *News of the*

World, and later with the *Daily Mirror*, in similar undercover investigations. Father Shay co-operated with all these enquiries and ironically the suspects from all three investigations – at separate times – headed out for the Philippines unaware that their moves were monitored, by Shay and us, and by the media.

The stories created a storm when they were released. *ITV News* delivered their undercover report over two nights with prominent coverage for Jubilee Campaign and an interview with me. This significant broadcast was probably the first time that a top British news programme had linked the key components of the issue. The news report demonstrated how easy it was for British sex tourists to abuse enslaved children without restrictions, and get away with it.

Some months afterwards, the *News of the World* splashed their story across the front page, and later the *Daily Mirror* reported the deeds of a university lecturer who travelled abroad regularly on such tours. These important stories, along with others, guaranteed that people were talking about the sex slavery business that trapped children for the exploitation of foreign tourists. The question on everyone's lips was: why doesn't the government do something about this scandal?

Parliamentary inaction

At the time, parliament was considering the Criminal Justice Bill and ECPAT persuaded Lord Archer of Sandwell QC, a former Solicitor General in the Labour government, to table our bill as an amendment to the Criminal Justice Bill, which was under review at the time.

Conservative government opposition ensured its failure, but Lord Hylton picked it up again in the House of Lords. On the day before the bill's second reading in parliament, Glenda Jackson MP delivered Jubilee's 20,000-strong petition calling for a change in the law to Downing Street and captured television and radio coverage in its support. Hours later, the government let it be known that it would oppose the passage of Hylton's bill in the Commons.

Their compromise was to consider prosecuting sex tour operators instead. Clearly someone had watched the *ITV News* story. In parliamentary code, this was the bill's death knell, but no one was surprised. The government had continued to argue that the bill was unworkable and predictable form letters sped off Whitehall's word processors to anyone who enquired. However, that argument was decisively squashed in June 1995, when a Swedish court successfully prosecuted a 69-year-old former civil servant, Bengt Bolin, for sexual intercourse with a 14-year-old boy while on holiday in Thailand on 18 February 1993.

While the media maintained its public pressure, the government was monitoring events unfolding behind the scenes in Ireland. Through separate high-level contacts, both Father Shay and Jubilee were able to reach top politicians in Ireland, and in November 1995 the Oireachtas (the Republic of Ireland parliament) endorsed the legislation. Owen Ryan, an active TD (Irish MP), told us, 'Child prostitution is a new form of slavery. It's outrageous that Irish citizens can be guilty of abusing children but escape punishment.'

In Britain, the brutal murder of nine-year-old Daniel Handley in east London in 1994 shocked the country after it was revealed that he had been sexually abused before the killing. His killers fled to the Philippines, but were tracked down by Father Shay following a request by the British police. I was in the Philippines when his investigators found evidence that the killers had been abusing children while in Olongapo. British detectives flew out after Father Shay's information was filed, but when the perpetrators were arrested, it was on an immigration offence. This case provided the most dramatic evidence yet of how sex tourists could travel with impunity, the ease with which they could conceal their movements and the fact that children were caught up in the exploitation, abuse and slavery.

Change at last

The increasing media coverage, followed by the Irish bill, and finally the Daniel Handley case, convinced the authorities that they had to act. The government did a sudden U-turn and announced that they would introduce extraterritorial jurisdiction laws. Much of the legislation, when it did come in 1997, was modelled on the bill that Jubilee Campaign's parliamentary officer Wilfred Wong had drafted two years earlier. At the same time, the government introduced a sex register for child sex offenders.

I was surprised that it had taken this long to convince the authorities and had assumed that things would change as soon as we told people that children were enslaved and exploited. Still, it was an important campaign and clearly demonstrated that as individuals we could make a difference when we used media coverage and political pressure backed by prayer and action.

Bombay nightmare

I wanted to find some practical way to help children trapped in child prostitution and sex slavery. On a visit to India in 1996, I was taken into the notorious red-light district of Bombay by a remarkable Christian missionary, Reverend K. K. Deveraj, who had won the trust of the sex workers, their families, the local community, even the brothel owners.

It was a nightmare world of crowded, claustrophobic streets, ramshackle wooden buildings with barred windows like prison cells. On the streets, girls of all ages loitered around, dressed in bright-coloured saris and dresses with sparkling bangles and heavily painted faces. Their eyes winked enticingly, but seemed strangely dead.

I talked to some of the girls and heard their stories first hand. Some had been enticed, lured, tricked, trafficked, others sold, some by friends or relatives, some by strangers. On entering the brothel, each one was held in a caged cell for about two to three weeks until their will was broken and the reality of their situation hit them. Most were raped, brutalised, beaten and forced to submit to the demands of the business. Some had physical scars; for others the wounds were emotional and would probably never heal. Controlled by violence and coercion, each one was trapped in a vicious debt bondage system; the girls were sold to the brothels and worked to pay off their debt, but no records were kept and many were hazy about the exact details of their debt or how much had been paid off. Customers paid the brothel and the girls survived on tips; in reality, it was a debt that could never really be repaid. Anyone trying to escape was beaten severely. Suicides were spoken of factually; no one knew anyone who had got away. If ever they could scrape up the money to pay off the brothel, their choices were few. Stigmatised by their circumstances, most knew they could never return home for the shame it would bring their family. Each girl was living out a life sentence in a place far from home.

Rescue mission

Reverend Deveraj introduced me to Asha and a few young girls, aged between 12 and 14, who were at risk from being sold into the sex industry. The girls trusted him and clung to some hope that he could do something to prevent their sale. Amidst the filth, squalor, corruption and oppression, the very presence of a slave kingdom, these girls seemed like jewels strewn in the rubbish.

I asked if Asha and the other girls could be rescued and was told the mission was possible, but a house would be needed outside Bombay. I returned home scorched and the experience haunted me day and night. I was determined to raise the money to establish a home – quite a lot for a small group like us. Remarkably, within a short space of time, the money was raised and the girls I had met had been rescued. Soon more were able to come out. All the girls were orphaned or abandoned children from the red-light district who had no way to escape from the sex slavery that had absorbed everything within reach. Once the news spread that a baby was being offered for sale in one of the brothels for £150. Our team heard about the sale and Reverend Deveraj raced to the area and was able to rescue the child. He named her Glory. Today she lives in one of our homes.

Our friends and supporters were just tremendous. The money came from various sources. Some were small, sacrificial gifts. One of the larger gifts was from Olivia and George Harrison, who both took a personal interest in the girls whom I had originally met and the mission to rescue children from sex slavery. When the *Beatles Anthology* was released, George suggested that a portion of the profits should go to charity, and our work in India was one of many to benefit. After George's sad passing, 'My Sweet Lord' was re-released with the profits going to good causes, and Olivia remembered us. The money paid for two years' running costs for a shelter we had started deep in the heart of Bombay's red-light district. It was open every day and night to give protection and help to the children of prostitutes.

Steve Brown, Billy Connolly's manager, introduced him to the work and it captured his heart. He donated one night's concert takings to us in 1997. It was a huge sum of money and we had the option of using it to pay for the running costs of our first home for one entire year. Instead, we built a second home and even more children were rescued. Billy and Steve launched Tickety-Boo Tea with the help of Nadeem Ahmed's company Global Tea & Commodities, and all the profits from the sale of the tea paid for the running costs of these homes for several years. But the pressure was turned up when companies like Tesco and Safeway were unable to give us shelf space for the 'chari-tea' and we were faced with the challenge of raising the operational costs of the homes.

The HIV/AIDS epidemic in India has been like a 'time bomb' ticking away beneath the surface. India has about five million people living with HIV/AIDS, the largest number in the Asia Pacific region and the second largest in the world after South Africa. The impact in Bombay's red-light district has been devastating. The police have frequently called Reverend Deveraj to ask for his assistance over a dead body in the sex district, as very few want to handle the victims of the disease. They know he is the only one they can rely on to deal with the consequences of the AIDS explosion.

Some of the girls who had been rescued had seen their mothers die from AIDS and a few were HIV-positive. Stirred by the situation, we took up the challenge to start another home for children orphaned by the disease.

My daughter Rachel had become a pen pal with one of the girls in our homes and donated some of her pocket money to the work. When she heard that we were planning to build a home for orphans, she decided to raise funds for this new project through a sky dive. Rachel's jump raised a phenomenal £75,000 from generous Jubilee supporters. With this massive donation we were able to get matched funding from the Laing Trust here in the UK and from a similar arrangement through Ann Buwalda and Jubilee Campaign in the US. As a result, we secured all the funds to build this new home and run it for three years. It was a powerful demonstration of the difference we can make with imagination and commitment.

Rachel spent a memorable week with the girls at our homes in Bombay and wrote this heartfelt poem on her return.

The Children Whom Life Forgot

In the bright sun these children play
The lucky few who got away
They were picked up, they were helped out
They were shown what life's all about
Here they are happy, here they run free
But they need no reminder of how their lives could have been
Before they were freed, their lives were a shock
These were the children whom life forgot

They once lived in hatred, in dirt and in fear
And if they cried for help, no one would hear
Their lives had no meaning, no future prepared
And in this vicious circle, no girl would be spared
For in any second, as time moves along
They'd be forced into the life which had just killed their mum
Then in the blink of an eye, their childhood is gone
There's no time for growing, as life must go on

And soon enough, they'll become masters of the trade
And have children whose life will be just the same

Imagine a life with no hope and no meaning
Imagine a house with no walls and no ceiling
Imagine being taught to expect nothing from life
Imagine waking each day to more pain and more strife
Imagine looking down the street, knowing that's all you've got
Imagine knowing you're the child whom life forgot

These few lucky children whose lives have been spared
Now live for a reason, their future's been paved
They carry a spirit, which cannot be measured
They live a rich life, which doesn't need treasures
They've learned life's big secrets, its lessons we're told
They know the life they're living is richer than gold
They now have a purpose, their name means a lot
They're no longer the children whom life forgot
For now, these bright children play under the sun
Their lives once forgotten have now just begun

The mission in India has been an extraordinary success, but it is still tough to keep the work going. Over 100 girls have been rescued or have taken refuge in one of our homes or shelters. Some of the older girls have moved on to further education or found employment. Asha, the first girl who was rescued, has married and had her first child, and has herself rescued others. It is an extraordinary triumph of faith and courage. If these children had not been rescued, every one of those girls would have become a twenty-first-century slave.

* * *

End this evil

Slavery is illegal globally – but the world's leading expert, Professor Kevin Bales, tells us in this book that there are more slaves alive today than all the slaves stolen from Africa over four centuries of the slave trade.

This is not a moment to celebrate, but a time to commit to put an end to this twenty-first-century evil. The first step on this journey is taken with a book such as this. Our hope and prayer is that *Slavery Now and Then* will inspire you to get involved. We can – and must – use our freedom to help those who are denied the same rights that we take for granted.

We can all play some part with our prayer, action and support. There is no other way. There is no 'Plan B'.

DANNY SMITH

Danny Smith lives in Surrey with his wife Joan and their three children, Jessica, Rachel and Luke. An Anglo-Indian, he has published widely on rock music and human rights. He is a co-founder, with David Alton, of Jubilee Campaign, a human rights pressure group with consultative status at the UN, and of the international human rights charity Jubilee Action, delivering practical help for children at risk.

To find out more, read Danny's book *Who Says You Can't Change the World?* or write for details on Jubilee's work. Visit the websites at www.jubileecampaign.co.uk and www.jubileeaction.co.uk.

If you are interested in supporting the girls rescued from slavery in India, e-mail Danny directly at danny@jubileecampaign.co.uk.

PART ONE: MODERN SLAVERY

No one shall be held in slavery or servitude; slavery and the slave trade shall be prohibited in all their forms.

Article 4, Universal Declaration of Human Rights

Slavery is a social and economic relationship defined by three criteria:

1. the complete control of one person, the slave, by another, using violence or the threat of violence to maintain that control;
2. the economic exploitation of the slave's labour;
3. no remuneration, beyond basic subsistence, for the exploited labour.

Slavery has taken and continues to take many forms across time and across cultures. These forms have been established and expressed through various combinations of law, religion, custom, economics, racism, criminality and armed conflict. Whatever the form of slavery, at its core are the three attributes of violent control, economic exploitation and no remuneration.

Professor Kevin Bales, President, Free the Slaves

1: How we will end slavery in the twenty-first century

Professor Kevin Bales, President,
Free the Slaves

It may seem mad, or the extreme of hubris, to assert that after more than 5,000 years of slavery, we will bring it to an end. Slavery has been a permanent part of the human existence throughout all of human history, but like smallpox or the burning of witches, its time is over. Human slavery may seem to be the immovable monolith, but it is actually a weak shell ready to topple. There will be pockets of resistance to ending slavery, but for most of the 27 million slaves in the world today the transition to citizenship and restored dignity is not just immediately possible, it is inevitable.

Fewer hurdles

There are a number of reasons why eradication is possible, and a favourable social, political and economic context provides a foundation. This can be seen in three key challenges that we do *not* have to face. The first is that we do not have to win the moral argument against slavery; no government or organised interest group is pressing the case that slavery is desirable or even acceptable. No priest or minister is standing in the pulpit and giving biblical justifications for slavery. No philosophers offer up rationalisations for slavery. In fact, with the exception of a handful of criminals, the world is united in its condemnation of slavery. The Universal Declaration of Human Rights simply underscores this, placing freedom from slavery at the top of the list of fundamental rights. The moral challenge today is how we can *act effectively* on our universally held belief in the absolute and essential equality of human dignity.

The second challenge that we do not have to face is the argument that slavery is necessary for our economic well-being. The actual monetary value of slavery in the world economy is extremely small. One estimate states that all the work done by slaves in the whole world in a year is worth about $13 billion, the same amount that spam e-mails cost the commercial world each year. A recent study by the United Nations estimated that global profits from human trafficking are about $31 billion a year. This sounds like a lot of money, and it is, but to put it into perspective, consumers in the United States are expected to spend $31 billion buying doors and windows in 2007. In the global economy this is a small drop in a large ocean. The end of slavery threatens the livelihood of no country or industry. No country can say, 'We would *like* to end slavery, but we just can't afford it.' In fact, just the opposite is true. While slaves may make money for slave holders, they are a drag on a country's economy. They contribute little to national production; their work is concentrated on the lowest rung of the economic ladder, doing low-skill jobs that are dirty and dangerous. Slaves work both ineffectively and as little as they can, and who can blame them? The value of their work is stolen and pocketed by criminals. Economically, except for the criminals, slaves are a waste. They contribute next to nothing to a country's economy; they buy nothing in a country's markets. They are actually an untapped economic resource.

In Northern India models of community-based liberation and

economic reintegration are being tested and polished. In more than 100 villages the story is the same: with only a little assistance freed slaves dramatically increase their incomes, and choose to invest immediately in education for their children, increasing their food consumption and health, and then buying assets that provide a livelihood such as land and livestock. For poor countries, significantly increasing the earning and spending of ex-slaves would be a small but important improvement in the national economy. At the international level, if you compare countries on the strength of their economy and how many slaves they have, the picture is clear: the more slaves, the weaker the economy. There is simply no economic reason to keep slavery alive.

The third great challenge that we do not have to face is the one celebrated by this book – the necessity to pass laws against slavery. For the most part, the laws needed to end slavery are already on the statute books. Around the world some of these laws need updating and expanding, and some need their penalties increased. Many anti-slavery laws are waiting for the allocation of funds needed to train police in their use. And given the international nature of human trafficking, nearly all these laws need to be brought into harmony with each other. Many improvements are needed, but there is nowhere on earth that slavery is legal. As we bring an end to slavery, in most cases we will need the political will to enforce law, not campaigns to make new law. The most important laws needing enactment are those appropriating funds needed for eradication.

How much will it cost to end slavery?

Let's go back to Northern India for an example of the cost of liberation. Debt bondage in South Asia accounts for as many as 10 million of the world's slaves. Since an enslaved family's work is considered collateral, not repayment of their loan, this form of slavery is often hereditary. It is not unusual to find families in their third and fourth generation of debt bondage slavery in

Northern India, completely unaware that a life in freedom is possible. All the worst features of slavery mark debt bondage: violence, rape, degradation, malnutrition and hopelessness. If we can crack this form of slavery, literally millions will come to freedom. The good news is that the programmes for liberation and reintegration are well developed and well tested. If we go back over several years and add together the costs of paying for the outreach workers and their transportation to rural villages, of organising, guaranteeing seed money and maintaining the micro-credit unions, of keeping the local organisation's office[1] ticking over, and so forth, then divide that sum by the number of families they help to freedom in a year, the result is about £19.

So, for the price of a nice lunch or a pair of blue jeans, a family goes from slavery to freedom. None of that money goes to pay off the illegal debt that holds the family in bondage, or to give money to criminals to 'buy' the slave's freedom. What it does include is the cost of helping the family achieve an independent life and getting their children to school. The project helps villagers to organise themselves and to know and safeguard their legal rights. It leads to families getting control of the means to earn an independent living. Freedom may be precious, but it does not have to be expensive.

The cost of freedom is important because governments run on money. It would be possible to look to individuals and charities to bankroll the end of slavery, but since every government agrees that slavery is a crime, and since practically every citizen of every country condemns slavery, could there be a better expression of our common will than to work through our elected governments? In any event, we have tried the gradual approach of asking charities to do this job, but now it is time to finish the job once and for all. The aim for our charitable giving, both as individuals

---

[1] This is the Sankalp Organisation that works in Uttar Pradesh. Sankalp works in partnership with the American anti-slavery organisation Free the Slaves. To know more about, and support, their work see www.freetheslaves.net.

and trusts, is to continue to support the work of liberation, but also to fund the work needed to bring governments fully into play. An increased emphasis on and support for increasing the participation of governments will leverage the funds needed for real eradication.

Knowing what it will cost to end slavery in a country makes it possible to build an effective strategy for eradication with meaningful government participation. Remarkably, the balance of costs and benefits for ending slavery makes it a great investment. Let's assume that the £19 figure for liberation and a new life works for slaves all over the world, not just in India. What would that mean in terms of the price of ending all slavery? If there are 27 million slaves, our best estimate, then ending slavery on the planet earth would cost £511 million. That is beyond the reach of human rights organisations, but it is one tenth of one per cent of the current annual budget of the UK government. Put another way, it is what the BBC spends on just the television programmes that it makes *outside* London. It works out to £8.45 per person in Great Britain. Freedom is not just affordable, it's a bargain. And there is no reason to assume that Britain has to pay the whole bill for eradication. Shared amongst the rich countries, the cost would be pennies per person – painless and possible.

These cost comparisons are important because they show that money is not the barrier to ending slavery. They demonstrate that with political will and a fairly small amount of input, eradication is achievable. Of course, it is true that freedom for many slaves will cost more than the £19 found in Northern India. Removing children from slavery in the fishing industry in Ghana seems to be costing £200 per child, for example, and helping people who have been trafficked into Europe and North America will be even more expensive. When the human traffickers linked to organised criminal gangs need to be caught and punished, the price will be even higher. These criminal networks are notoriously hard to crack. Likewise, there are many parts of the world where the poverty that increases the vulnerability to slavery is so acute that fundamental changes will need to be made. Then there are the governments that are tacitly supporting slavery, exploiting their own citizens as forced labour. These unelected dictatorships, as 'sovereign nations', will require expensive diplomatic and economic leverage. But even if the cost of global freedom doubles or triples, it is still a relatively small sum, an infinitesimally small fraction of the global economy. And, as we have seen, stable and sustainable freedom generates economic growth and thus pays for itself.

If we can afford it, how do we actually do it?

The abolitionists of the past had the great benefit of a precise goal – passing a law to make slavery illegal. We will never have that luxury; there is no magic bullet that will eradicate slavery, but there are many known avenues to freedom. While the basic conditions of slavery are fundamentally the same the world over, every slave lives and suffers in a unique situation. The social, cultural, political, economic and sometimes religious packaging that is wrapped around slavery in different countries and cultures means that our eradication methods will tend to follow general patterns that are then adapted to each unique setting. While some slaves can be freed individually, in some cases whole communities need to be freed together to ensure a sustainable liberation.

One avenue leads us to think hard about the products we buy that are tainted with slavery. None of us like the fact that cotton, cocoa, sugar, steel, even some of the metal in mobile phones and computers, may have been produced with slavery. The total volume of these slave-made commodities is actually very small. Only a tiny fraction of the world's cotton or cocoa or steel has slave input. The problem is that it is almost impossible to know which shirt or chocolate bar or chair carries slavery into your home. The criminals using slaves sell their produce into the market like everyone else, and it flows into the global market and mixes with the products of free workers. While the criminals may justify their use of slaves by pointing to economic pressures to reduce labour costs, they never pass the savings from slavery to the consumer. The slave holder pockets the market price for his slave-made goods – a price set in a market that reflects the presence of free workers. So, if slave holders are feeding on our purchases, it would seem that we should just stop buying those goods. In fact, that may be exactly the wrong thing to do.

The revulsion we feel when we think we are eating something or wearing something that comes from slave labour is strong. Our reaction is to push that crime away from us, to distance ourselves. The last thing we want to do is support slave holders in their crime. Yet, for every criminal using slaves to grow cocoa or cotton or sugar, there are hundreds or thousands of farmers producing the same crops without using slaves. Great agribusinesses are involved and every size of farm in between. Small farmers in the developing world have enough problems competing against the vast subsidies given to US and European agribusiness; if the consumers turn against them as well, the result could be destitution and potentially enslavement. So, while our disgust says, 'Boycott!' the truth is that boycotts can hurt the innocent more than the guilty. We think of ourselves as consumers. We want to vote in the marketplace for the things we believe in. But this problem cannot normally be fixed at the point of purchase.

Let's follow the path of a shirt tainted with slave-grown cotton. The point of purchase is the last stop in a long line from the farm to you. The cotton grown and picked with slave labour piles up at the cotton gin with all the other cotton for processing. Packed into bales, the ginned cotton, now a mixture of 'free' and 'slave' cotton, moves to a factory for carding, spinning and weaving. That factory may be in another country or even another continent. The product chain stretches out and over borders: spun thread is made into cloth, which goes to a mill for dying or printing; then from mill to factory for cutting and sewing; then from factory to distribution centre for packaging and shipping; finally it reaches a wholesaler who sends it to the retail shop where you find it on the rack. Behind that shirt are the truck drivers and salespeople, the seamstresses, the mill and factory hands, the gin workers, and the transport workers who drove the raw cotton to the gin. At the beginning of the chain are lots of farmers and a handful of slaves. Along this chain, some of the workers are paid well, some are being exploited, and some are not paid at all. Boycotting that shirt can hurt them all.

The place to stop slavery is not at the cash register; it has to be stopped where it happens – on the farm, at the quarry, or in the sweatshop. The £20 you don't spend boycotting a shirt is worth little or nothing to the fight against slavery. The slave holder has already had his profit on the front end, and if boycott leads to a collapse in cotton prices, the slave holder just moves his slaves to another job, or dumps them, or worse. Meanwhile, boycott-driven unemployment puts other farmers and mill hands at risk of enslavement. A boycott is a blunt instrument: sometimes it is exactly the right tool, but often it runs the risk of creating more suffering than it cures. Sometimes the immediate and obvious answer is not the right one.

Fortunately, there is another way that is more effective. If companies work with anti-slavery groups, taking responsibility for their product chains and establishing systems that root out slavery at the farm gate, then the slavery can be removed from the product at its source. To take the slavery out of cotton or cocoa or any other product, you have to set slaves free and bust the criminals who enslave them. You also have to crack the system feeding slavery into the product chain; otherwise criminals will just suck more people into slavery. Once they are freed, ex-slaves need support to build independent, stable lives. Here the circle closes and the way ahead becomes clearer. The £20 you might spend on a shirt is the cost of freeing a family in Northern India. Don't stop buying shirts, just start investing in freedom and urging businesses to join with consumers, churches and governments in ending slavery for good.

WHERE ARE MOST OF THE WORLD'S SLAVES?

People can be held in slavery in any country. The majority of the world's slaves are in South Asia (India, Pakistan, Bangladesh and Nepal). These people are held in debt bondage/bonded labour, a system in which a person becomes bonded by accepting a loan from a moneylender, which they must work to repay. Workers are then tricked or trapped into labouring for little or no pay, under conditions that violate their human rights, from which they cannot escape. Most of these slaves work in agriculture, brick making, or other industries that feed into the local economy of their country. Other slaves are bonded into working at factories that produce export items for Western Europe and North America and the global market, such as oriental rugs, diamonds and silk. Africa and South America both have large numbers of slaves in some areas, and the recent increase in human trafficking is bringing slavery to many countries in Europe, North America and Southeast Asia.

IS THERE SLAVERY IN THE UNITED STATES?

There is slavery in the United States, mostly due to human trafficking for domestic work, migrant farm labour, or enslavement in prostitution. Migrant workers are tricked into working for little or no pay as means of repayment for debts from their transport into the US, similar to debt bondage in South Asia. Domestic workers and women and children forced into prostitution are trafficked into the US with promises of jobs and education and then held as slaves. The US government estimates that 14,500–17,500 people are trafficked into the US each year, and the total number of slaves in the US may be as high as 40,000.[2]

---

[2] Information courtesy of Free the Slaves.

Using our role as consumers is just one way ahead. If we start at the grass roots and work up, we can see many more ways to stop slavery. At the level of farms and villages there are individuals risking their lives to help others out of slavery. There are also the local anti-slavery and human rights organisations that support these workers. To increase their impact and free more slaves, at least three things need to happen. The first is that local anti-slavery workers need to be protected. There are martyrs today, people we never hear about. Those of us who live in the rich North need to keep reminding governments that these heroes are the sharp end of the tool that breaks chains and they deserve our support. The second thing needed at the grass roots is the money to expand those programmes that are successful. Careful tracking shows efficient and powerful local programmes on every continent, and nearly every one of these is limping along on a shoestring. This borders on criminal neglect. If there are slaves in front of us and we know an efficient way to liberation, then we need to put our money where our mouths are. Third, we need to clone the liberators. It is a perfectly reasonable goal to say, 'Where there is one liberator today, there will be three next year.' In spite of the danger, there is no shortage of people ready to do this work. This is simply a resource question. We need to find the best anti-slavery workers and then invest in giving them apprentices, extending their reach and activity. Every one of these points can be achieved, to use organisation-speak, through good human resource management.

Supporting individual anti-slavery workers is not the way to end slavery for good, but it is the job that needs doing now. These liberators are like the emergency aid workers fighting an epidemic. For every epidemic research is needed; health policies have to change; the whole public health system of sewers, water treatment and hospitals needs to be rebuilt; but when people are starting to die *today* someone needs to deliver the vaccine and the food *today*. Today there are slaves waiting to be freed. As we begin the long process of turning the giant supertankers of government

SLAVERY NOW – AND THEN

and building the international alliance against slavery, these grass-roots workers are all that usually stands between slaves and a lifetime of slavery.

At the level of governments, two related and achievable actions will take place in the next five to ten years. I say this with a degree of certainty, because law-makers in many countries of the rich North are already preparing to move ahead. The first action is that the rich countries will devote the necessary diplomatic and financial resources to make the end of slavery a priority. There are many carrots and a few sticks that might be offered to countries that continue to have high levels of slavery. The second is that some of these resources will be directed to the global South to support the enforcement of local laws against slavery and the establishment of sustainable lives for ex-slaves. Remember that the total number of slaves in the world means that this is a problem within our collective and governmental grasp, if we choose to reach for it. The US, for example, has recently given other countries more than $2 billion to help them better enforce anti-drug laws. It is a pattern easily replicated for anti-slavery laws.

At the international level other existing patterns of research, policy, diplomacy and outreach can easily be transferred to ending slavery. We know that when governments really get involved in collective international efforts, big changes can happen. In 1988 the Global Polio Eradication campaign began, with nearly every government in the world promising to take part. In that year, the crippling polio disease was active in 125 countries. By 2003 there were only six countries left with active polio. As with many diseases, it will be difficult to wipe out the polio virus completely, but the campaign has saved millions of children and adults from being crippled by the disease. Slavery can also go from being global, pernicious and pervasive to being a rare crime on the watch list.

We are all familiar with the role of UN weapons inspectors. Their job has been to ensure that countries are keeping the promises they have made when ratifying UN conventions on weapons of mass destruction. Given that essentially every country in the world has ratified the various UN anti-slavery conventions, and that prohibitions against slavery have been ruled to be universal and fundamental by international courts, it is perfectly reasonable to establish UN slavery inspectors. Their job would be to help countries identify and correct holes in the enforcement of their own laws and their international commitments.

Notice that none of these steps require any radical new approaches or rules. Existing structures, tools and methods simply need to be turned with sufficient focus and resource to push slavery into the waste bin with polio.

Life after slavery – no freedom without forgiveness?

No other country in the world so dramatically demonstrates the consequences of a botched emancipation as the United States. America has suffered, and continues to suffer, from the injustice perpetrated on ex-slaves. Generations of African-Americans were sentenced to second-class status, exploited, denied and abused. Without education and basic resources, it was very difficult for African-American families to build the economic foundation needed for full participation and well-being in America. Today there are laws that have criminals make restitution for what they have stolen, for the damage they have inflicted. No such restitution came for the stolen lives of millions of slaves.

At the end of the American Civil War, nearly four million ex-slaves were dumped into the society and economy of the United States with little preparation. Today there are some 27 million slaves in the world. If we can end slavery in this generation, which is a real possibility, do we really want the next four, five, or twenty generations to face the problems of emancipation gone wrong? Our aim in ending slavery cannot be the creation of a population whose suffering and anger spills out over the decades. Helping freed slaves achieve full lives is one of the best investments a government or a society can make. We know the alternative; that way lies a horrible waste of human potential. It also gives birth to anger, retribution, vengeance, hatred and violence. In fact, one of the most profound questions about slavery and freedom that remains unanswered is this: even if there is restitution, can there be forgiveness?

Those who have suffered enslavement may well say that this is a crime beyond forgiveness. It is no momentary act of violence, no crime of passion, but a systematic brutality and exploitation that can stretch over generations. It combines within itself the most horrible crimes known – torture, rape, kidnap, murder, and the wilful destruction of the human mind and spirit. It is exploitation, injustice and violence all rolled together into their most potent forms. The damage it does and has done is inestimable – a damage that includes the minds deeply injured by enslavement.

The minds injured by slavery include the minds of the slave holders. By dehumanising another person in order to enslave them, the slave holder dehumanises himself. Those of us with little direct experience of slavery find it hard to feel any concern for the slave holder, but many of those who have lived in slavery recognise the damage slavery does to the master as well. A community that allows slavery in its midst is sick to its roots. For the ex-slave to grow as a citizen, that sickness needs to be treated, especially because many freed slaves live in the same area where they were enslaved. Ex-slaves and their slave holders may see each other regularly. If injustices are allowed to fester, it will be impossible for either group to move on. In America, the ugly sickness of slavery re-emerged in segregation, discrimination and lynch law. In part, this was because most Americans sought to ignore the legacy of slavery. The immediate needs of freed slaves were not met in the years following 1865, and ever since there has been an attempt to draw a curtain over the past, to let bygones be bygones.

We can see a parallel in post-apartheid South Africa. Faced with the large-scale horrific murders and torture of the past, many people in that country argued that collective amnesia would best serve the reconstruction of a truly democratic state. But, as Desmond Tutu explained, 'Our common experience in fact is the opposite – that the past, far from disappearing or lying down and being quiet, is embarrassingly persistent, and will return and haunt us unless it has been dealt with adequately. Unless we look the beast in the eye we will find that it returns to hold us hostage.'[3] In America that beast has been on the prowl for more than 100 years, and has evolved into new forms of discrimination, recrimination and injustice. Putting down that beast is one of America's greatest challenges. Ensuring that the same beast never grows up when slaves are freed today is a challenge for the whole world.

To ensure that freed slaves build new lives, and that communities overcome the sickness of slavery, to find the best ways to liberate slaves and to help governments enforce their own anti-slavery laws, means building a sound understanding of what slavery is today and discovering best points of intervention. We cannot solve a problem we do not understand. This brief essay has explored only a fraction of the avenues to freedom that will take us to a world without slavery. If we really want to end slavery we have to get past outrage and focus on analysis, then build practical tools and solutions from that analysis without stinting on resources. We stand at a moment in human history when our economies, governments, understanding, moral beliefs and hearts are aligned in a constellation that can bring slavery to an end. Will this be our gift to our children and their children, or just another missed opportunity?

KEVIN BALES
Kevin Bales is president of Free the Slaves (www.freetheslaves.net), the US sister organisation of Anti-Slavery International, and professor of sociology at Roehampton University, London. He is also a trustee of Anti-Slavery International. His book *Disposable People: New Slavery in the Global Economy* was nominated for a Pulitzer Prize and published in ten languages. Desmond Tutu

[3] Desmond Tutu, *No Future Without Forgiveness* (London: Rider, 1999), p. 31.

SLAVERY NOW – AND THEN

called it 'a well researched, scholarly and deeply disturbing exposé of modern slavery'. In 2006 his work was named one of the top '100 World-Changing Discoveries' by the association of British universities. He won the Premio Viareggio for services to humanity in 2000. The film based on his book, which he co-wrote (*Slavery*, by Kate Blewett and Brian Woods of True Vision TV), won a Peabody Award and two Emmy Awards. He was awarded the Laura Smith Davenport Human Rights Award in 2005; the Judith Sargeant Murray Award for Human Rights in 2004; and the Human Rights Award of the University of Alberta in 2003. He was a consultant to the UN Global Programme on Human Trafficking. Bales has advised the US, British, Irish, Norwegian and Nepali governments, as well as the Economic Community of West African States, on slavery and human trafficking policy. In 2005 he published *Understanding Global Slavery*, and he is currently writing a book that lays out a road map for the global eradication of slavery. He gained his PhD at the London School of Economics.

2: Sudan: Slaughter and slavery

Baroness Cox of Queensbury,
The Humanitarian Aid Relief Trust (HART)

The bodies were piled high, rotting. The stench was overpowering. I was in a place of sheer carnage – human bodies, cattle corpses, burned homes, scorched-earth policy.

It was not my first time in Sudan, nor was it the first time I had seen human suffering. But in terms of the scale of horror and depression, my visit to Bahr-el-Gazal in Sudan just a few days after the National Islamic Front regime's forces had swept through the area, slaughtering civilians and burning villages, was one of my worst. Eighty men and two women had been killed, and their bodies were in a mass grave. At least 282 women and children had been abducted into slavery.

Perhaps even more challenging than the visual evidence of man's barbaric inhumanity to man were the words of a Catholic catechist whose brother and brother-in-law had been killed and whose sister had been captured as a slave. His church had been attacked, Bibles burned and homes, cattle, crops all destroyed. He told me that while the Sudanese regime spends a million dollars a day on the war, the Christians have nothing. 'Worse than that, we feel completely on our own. You are the only Christians who have even visited us for years,' he said. Then came the words that turned the knife in my heart. 'Doesn't the church want us any more?' asked the catechist. That is a question the church in the comfortable West needs to answer.

On that particular visit, I was accompanied by an experienced television journalist. He had seen war, poverty, death and destruction before, as I had. But after what we had witnessed in Bahr-el-Gazal, all we could do was weep. He sat by the river and wept. I sat under a tree and wept. It challenged my faith deeply. If we believe in a God of love, how could such carnage occur? Then I reflected on the birth of our Lord and Saviour. While we in the free, comfortable Western world celebrate Christmas with its material comforts, food, presents and Christmas tree-life, we often choose to forget the massacre of the innocents.

The challenge

My relationship with Sudan began on Christmas Day, 1985. I had been involved with activities behind the Iron Curtain, particularly travelling with trucks taking medical aid to Poland, for some years. As a nurse, I am deeply committed to humanitarian aid. As a social scientist, I believe that those of us who have the privilege of freedom have a responsibility to use it to speak up on behalf of those who are denied freedom. But I was not looking for adventures in the African desert and bushlands – until Christmas 1985, when a card arrived with a Sudan postmark.

My son Jonathan, who was 23 at the time, had felt called to work as a nurse in the developing world and so, after qualifying at the London Hospital, he joined the Fellowship for African Relief, part of Emmanuel International, as a missionary nurse in Sudan. Jonathan's card carried not just greetings and personal news, but a description of the humanitarian disaster in the country and concern that some of the medical projects he was involved in were in danger of collapse because of a desperate shortage of nurses. I read those words, and I instinctively knew God was giving me a challenge. I replied, offering my services as a nurse the following summer. To my surprise, Emmanuel International accepted my application, and I was soon packed off to the desert. Those in charge either thought I was dispensable, or else tough enough, because they dispatched me to their most difficult project, a health education programme in Hamrat-el-Wiz, north Kordofan. I learned some basic Arabic, ate sheep's intestines, had to have a flying beetle removed from my ear before it perforated my ear drum, rode for several hours on a camel, and slept under the stars in the desert.

Crimes against humanity

Since the National Islamic Front (NIF) regime took power by military coup in 1989 and began its jihad (holy war) against all who oppose it, I have made over 28 visits to Sudan – to Bahr-el-Gazal in the west, the Nuba Mountains in the middle, Southern Blue Nile and Western Upper Nile areas, and the Beja people in the east. I have seen the human tragedy – two million dead, five million displaced – unfold before my eyes, and with the West's compliance. I have deliberately travelled to the 'no-go' areas, because they are the places where the people are most in need, most cut off, most forgotten. Their stories need to be heard and they desperately need humanitarian support. The NIF regime would not allow access to these areas for the big international aid agencies – UN Operation Lifeline Sudan, the International Committee of the Red Cross (ICRC) and others – and so it is left to small, flexible charities and individuals to go in. The Sudanese regime has passed a prison sentence on me, which I often say I serve 'in absentia', and has threatened to shoot me out of the sky if they catch me flying in, but I believe it is vital to keep going. If we did not go to the 'no-go' zones, the people there would die of starvation, disease and bombardment unheard, unknown, unreached. When the laws of a land conflict with God's laws, I know which laws one should follow – and I do not believe it is God's laws that cut people off from aid and advocacy.

The NIF regime survives in power solely and simply through

military force. The jihad it has launched against all who oppose it has been jihad in its most brutal, most violent form, with slavery at its heart.

The attention of the world has in recent years been focused on Darfur, and rightly so. The genocide in Darfur is appalling. But similar crimes against humanity have been taking place for years in southern Sudan, until a precarious ceasefire agreement was signed in early 2005.

Typically, in the military offensives, the men were killed, while the women and children were taken as slaves. I have met hundreds of former slaves, and from their stories it is clear that slavery is a weapon of war in the hands of the regime. It is not simply an unfortunate consequence, as some might wish to think, but rather a deliberate strategy designed to fulfil the objectives of this jihad – the destruction of African communities and culture by the Sudanese Arabs, the forced Islamisation of the non-Muslim parts of Sudan, and the forced Arabisation of Sudanese Africans. Local Arab tribesmen have been mobilised to participate in the jihad by the NIF regime and told that instead of money as payment, they could keep the bounty of war as their reward – including the human bounty of slaves. Armed and equipped by the regime, they carried out slave raids, accompanied by government troops, on a massive scale.

The slaves' stories

Little Deng's story speaks for the slaves of Sudan. He was about ten years old when I met him. As I sat with him under a tree in southern Sudan, he told me how he had just been brought home from the north of Sudan by Arab traders who bring their cattle south in the dry season. They are friends of the African Dinka people and risk a great deal to try to find, buy back and bring back men, women and children who have been abducted and taken into slavery. On this occasion, they brought back several hundred slaves, including little Deng. He was traumatised, because he had just discovered that in the raid in which he was captured, two years previously, both his parents were killed. So he had just learned that he was an orphan. He wept. However, towards the end of our talk, I got a wistful little smile from Deng, who said, 'At least I am home again now. I am called by my own name, Deng [the Dinka word for 'rain', which is precious, so it means someone to be cherished]. At least I am no longer called Abd [the Arabic for 'slave'].'

One woman's story is typical. Aged 38, she was captured along with her three children when armed raiders came to her village on horseback. They were forced to walk for ten days. There were over 1,000 other people captured from different areas. They were fed bones and leftovers. They were not given enough water and so they relied on the leaves of trees for fluid. They were tied together at night, and given Arabic names. They were forced to observe Islamic practices, including attending the mosque, and they were beaten when they refused. She was raped, and conceived a child by her owner.

Malek, aged 13, was taken by 25 armed raiders while he was looking after his cattle. They took him, his mother, three brothers, five sisters and his 20 cows, and killed his father. When he refused to go, they beat him. He was forced to join the others, and they were tied together and forced to walk to Chatap, a journey of ten days. He was given the Muslim name Mohammed.

Abuk Marou Keer was blind. She was captured in a raid, and forced to walk 18 miles to a labour camp. She told me how she was almost strangled by her captors, and herded along with other slaves, beaten regularly, and forced to carry the bounty the raiders had looted. She was raped. 'The soldiers said this was retaliation for the death of one of their leaders in the raid against Nyamlell,' she told me. The captives were forced to grind grain from sunrise to sunset. All they were permitted to eat was the leftover waste grain. They were beaten and whipped.

Apin Apin Akot's wife and two daughters, Akec, aged nine, and Afaar, aged four, were taken in a raid. This tall, dignified Dinka farmer from Sokabat, a two-hour walk from Nyamlell, told me what happened. 'Hundreds of men on horseback charged on people and we ran away in panic. My wife was taken, and my children too. I was powerless to do anything.' The four-year-old girl, unable to keep up with the others, was tied by her abductor to his horse and dragged behind. Her left leg was paralysed as a result.

Desperate to find and free his family, Apin Apin Akot sold his cattle for $900, and headed north in pursuit of the raiders. He wanted to buy back his wife and children. For months he searched, and worked at the same time, saving the money he needed. Eventually he had the 150,000 Sudanese pounds he needed – the equivalent of 40 cattle. He bribed an Arab informer to take him to the man who now 'owned' his wife and daughters. The 'owner' was amazed to see him – but agreed to sell him back his wife and younger daughter. But he refused to give the nine-year-old girl back, for he wanted to keep her as a concubine. If Apin Apin Akot wanted her too, he would have to give another 50,000 Sudanese pounds. Apin Apin Akot had no more funds, and had to leave his distraught daughter behind. She sobbed, but held out some hope. 'The worst thing for me would be to die. As long as I stay alive, I know you will come for me.'

When we met Mr Apin Apin Akot, we gave him the money he needed to buy back his daughter. On a subsequent visit, a very happy father came running towards us, exclaiming, 'Every morning when I wake up I thank God because I could rescue my daughter and now we are together again as a family.'

Sometimes the slaves can be rescued, at great cost. But often they are lost for ever – or, if they resist, they are killed. I remember one brave man who tried to stop the raiders taking a boy into slavery. He was shot in the face at point-blank range with an automatic rifle. This happened in a 'no-go' area, and so the International Committee of the Red Cross could not rescue him. We were able to provide funds to evacuate him and other casualties whom we met just a few hours after the raid – but he died subsequently. Many remain unreached and untreated.

Abandoned by the world

Slavery in Sudan is well documented. Anti-Slavery International has compiled a formidable catalogue of evidence. The Rift Valley Institute has identified and interviewed more than 12,000 people who had been violently abducted from southern Sudan between 1983 and 2002. It also estimates that over 11,000 of those abducted have still not been accounted for. Between 1999 and 2004, the Commission for the Eradication of the Abduction of Women and Children (CEAWC) has rescued 2,628 former slaves and reunited them with their families. But over 10,000 are still waiting to be returned to their homes. So far, no one has been prosecuted for conducting slave raids.

I have seen the bombing and strafing by the regime's helicopter gunships and Russian-built Antonov bombers several times. On one occasion, the noise of an Antonov drowned out my interview with Thomas Cirillo, a commander of the Sudan People's Liberation Army (SPLA), the southern Sudanese soldiers fighting the NIF regime. We sought shelter in a foxhole, our heads just above ground, while the sound of gunfire and artillery shells filled the air. Eight people died and three were wounded in that one attack.

Commander Cirillo, a committed Christian, told me why he was fighting. He said that before every battle, the regime's troops shouted threats through loudspeakers. 'We will force you to become Muslims, whether you want to or not,' they would shout. In words that echoed the catechist's quoted earlier, Commander Cirillo said, 'Our struggle is not against Islam or against Muslims, but against a fundamentalist regime that wants to destroy our African heritage and faith. It is discouraging to see the Islamic fundamentalist government in Khartoum receive moral and material support from other Islamic countries, while we receive no support from the Christian world. Even their personnel are coming and fighting us. But we will continue in our struggle for freedom, even if we are forsaken by Christendom. We will die for our faith, and we will die as Christians. But please help my wounded – we have nothing.'

The feeling that they have been abandoned by the rest of the world is one shared by most people I have met in Sudan. I will never forget landing in Nyamlell, an area closed to international aid agencies. The Sudanese regime had forbidden Non-Governmental Organisations (NGOs) from working in this area – I did not believe the order was consistent with God's commands, and so it was one that I ignored. As we landed, people came running up to us. 'Thank God you have come,' they said. 'We thought the world had forgotten us.'

Faith and hope

Yet, as is the case throughout the world, in the midst of unimaginable suffering, and despite their feeling forgotten, we find incredible faith, courage, dignity, graciousness and hope. At the end of one visit to southern Sudan, I watched with some relief as our little plane landed on the tiny airstrip to take us back to Kenya and home. It could not stay on the ground for long, because if it were detected by the Sudanese regime's Antonov bombers, it would undoubtedly be blown up – either on the ground, as a sitting duck, or in the air. So as it landed, I lined my camera up to take a quick photograph, before getting ready to board and take off again. When I lined my camera up, all that was in view was empty bush and the little plane. But out of nowhere there appeared in the photograph a Dinka boy, carrying a cross. It symbolises the spirit, and the suffering, of the people of Sudan and the persecuted church worldwide – enslaved, tortured, starving, imprisoned, martyred, yet carrying the cross for the rest of us.

I had the great privilege of accompanying the exiled Catholic bishop of El-Obeid, Bishop Macram Gassis, on an illegal visit inside southern Sudan. As he greeted his people, he celebrated mass under the shade of a tamarind tree. Many of the people had no clothes and no food. Many had been slaves. To them he said these inspiring and challenging words.

'This most beautiful cathedral, not built with human hands, but by nature and by God, is filled with the people of God. We must tell our brothers and sisters that the people here are still full of hope and that they still smile, in spite of suffering and persecution. Your people have suffered slavery, but you are not slaves to the world but children of God who has told us we can call him "Abba, Father". Christianity gives us liberty; therefore we are no longer slaves, but free: children of liberty, freedom and truth. But we live in a bad world. Many of your people have been sold into slavery. But that is not to become a slave . . . The real slave is a slave to sin; who does injustice to brothers and sisters; who kills them. Some people feel naked because they have no clothes and they try to cover themselves because of their embarrassment. But this is not real nakedness. True nakedness is to be without love. Therefore be clothed in love. This is Christianity.'

The work goes on

Two hundred years ago, William Wilberforce introduced legislation to abolish the slave trade in this country. His commitment, dedication, persistence, courage and hard work are rightly celebrated. But let us never allow ourselves to indulge in the false confidence that Wilberforce's work is done. He and others ended the slave trade in this country, and rightly so, but the slave trade lives on in Sudan and elsewhere, and Wilberforce's fight continues. Slavery in Sudan has been documented by Amnesty International, Human Rights Watch and Anti-Slavery International, among others. Amnesty International confirmed that the Sudanese regime had 'abducted thousands of civilians, mostly women and children, and forced them into unpaid labour in the north, in effect turning them into slaves'. The same pattern is unfolding now in Darfur, with the Janjaweed's reign of terror, and yet still the world fails to act. International prayer and protest brought down apartheid – why are we so silent and passive about slavery?

Baroness Cox of Queensbury

Caroline Cox serves as chief executive of HART (Humanitarian Aid Relief Trust) and spends much of her time on international humanitarian work, having served as a non-executive director of the Andrei Sakharov Foundation, and as a trustee of MERLIN (Medical Emergency Relief International) and the Siberian Medical University. She is a patron or trustee of various other charities.

She served as a deputy speaker of the House of Lords from 1985 to 2005, and was founder chancellor of Bournemouth University. She is a vice president of the Royal College of Nursing and founding chancellor of Liverpool Hope University – Britain's first Christian ecumenical university; and a vice president of the Liverpool School of Tropical Medicine.

Lady Cox has been honoured with the Wilberforce Award and the International Mother Teresa Award. She has made many missions to conflict zones, including the Armenian enclave of Nagorno Karabakh, Sudan, Nigeria, Burma and Indonesia. She has also been instrumental in helping to change the former Soviet Union policies for orphaned and abandoned children from institutional to foster family care. In 2004 she was appointed as special representative for the Foreign and Commonwealth Office Freedom of Religion Panel.

She is the co-author of *This Immoral Trade: Slavery in the 21st Century*.

Find out more about Baroness Cox's work at www.hart-uk.org.

3: Human trafficking

Mike Kaye, Anti-Slavery International

An overview of trafficking in people

Trafficking takes place when violence, deception or coercion is used in order to move people away from their homes for the purposes of forced labour, servitude and other slavery-like practices. It is fundamentally different from smuggling, in which a person is assisted to cross a border illegally for a fee, but they are not subsequently exploited.

Trafficking occurs within and across national borders and is an extremely lucrative form of international crime. Due to the clandestine nature of trafficking, it is very difficult to say exactly how many people are trafficked, but the International Labour Organisation (ILO) estimates that there are some 2.5 million people who are victims of trafficking around the world.

People generally put themselves or their children in the hands of traffickers in order to improve their lives or to escape poverty, discrimination and conflict. They are typically promised well-paid jobs, better lifestyles or further education. Many think they will be able to send money back to their families. In reality they become forced labourers.

Traffickers seek out their victims in many different ways. Individuals may be approached directly with promises of well-paying jobs or through recruitment agencies, which offer to find them employment and make the travel arrangements. In other cases women are coerced into prostitution by their 'boyfriends'. Children may be abducted or sent away with their family's consent, as the family believe that their children will be well looked after and have better opportunities abroad than at home, particularly in relation to accessing education.

The initial cost of the travel is normally covered by the trafficker, or money is borrowed from family, friends or loan sharks. In either case, the trafficked person enters into a situation of debt. Once they arrive at their destination, they discover that the job they were promised does not exist, but they still have a debt to pay back, which can be anything between $1,000 and $35,000. This amount can then be inflated through charges for accommodation, food and interest on the loan they borrowed.

The debt itself, and the fact that they are in an unfamiliar place where they do not speak the language, leaves the trafficked person in a vulnerable position. In addition, traffickers frequently take away passports or other travel documents and tell their victims that if they go to the police they will be arrested, as they are in the country illegally. If this is not sufficient to make them submit to the trafficker's demands, then threats, violence, torture and rape can also be used. Traffickers also make threats of violence against friends and family in their country of origin as an effective way of ensuring that their victims keep working and do not try to escape.

Men, women and children are all trafficked. Roughly a third of trafficked people are used exclusively for labour exploitation (e.g. domestic work, agricultural work, catering, packing and processing, etc.). Trafficking for sexual exploitation almost exclusively affects women and girls, but trafficking for labour exploitation also affects more women than men. Every continent and most countries are affected by trafficking, as highlighted by the examples below.

Trafficking in Indonesia

Poverty, high unemployment and a lack of formal education opportunities are driving increasing numbers of Indonesian women to migrate abroad into informal employment sectors such as domestic work.

Immigration restrictions and traditional constraints on women travelling on their own or looking for work abroad make Indonesian migrant women more dependent on third parties and, therefore, more vulnerable to being exploited. Indonesians wishing to work abroad as domestics are legally required to go through private recruitment agencies. Some agencies are responsible for human rights abuses within Indonesia, as well as for trafficking women to other countries.

The agencies send prospective migrant domestic workers to training camps for several months, or even up to a year. The women are not allowed to leave the camps and are often forced to work for the agency staff, carrying out domestic tasks in the camps. They are compelled to sign contracts, which may be in other languages. Physical and sexual abuses have been reported.

Hundreds of these camps exist in Indonesia, with no basic standards, government inspection or regulation. 'Recruitment' and 'harbouring' fall under the internationally accepted UN definition of trafficking, so these abuses are part of the trafficking process.

When these women eventually arrive at their employment destinations – typically Hong Kong, Taiwan, Malaysia, or one of the Gulf States – they are not normally paid anything for between five and seven months, during which time they have to pay back the extortionate agency fees (from around $2,500). Even if a woman is mistreated she cannot leave, because of the contract she was forced to sign and the money she 'owes' to the agency.

Adek went to a broker in her town to help her go to Hong Kong, because she had heard from a relative that she could get a better job there for more money. The broker took Adek to an employment agency in Surabaya, East Java, where she had to pay 390,000 *rupias* ($44) for a medical test, uniform, Cantonese language books and cookery books.

Instead of going straight to Hong Kong as she expected, Adek was sent to a training camp in Surabaya. There were around 1,000 women in this camp and conditions were bad. The women were served small portions of food and the water was dirty; many women in the camp were ill as a result. While Adek was there one woman died through lack of medical care. Adek and the other women were forced to carry out tasks for the agency staff, including cleaning duties, and to undertake long hours of language tuition.

Adek was not allowed to go outside the camp. Her family was only allowed to visit her for a few hours once every two weeks. Adek was forced to sign contract papers without any explanation as to what the contract entailed. After four months, she was taken to Hong Kong to begin her employment, but she was not paid anything for five months. She was told that this was to repay the agency fees she owed. Adek faced routine verbal abuse, was not allowed to leave the apartment and had only one rest day in nine months of employment.

Trafficking in Russia

Trafficking affects thousands of women and men in Russia. Women are trafficked from all over the country and forced to work as prostitutes or domestic workers. Men are trafficked into agricultural or construction work. They are taken to countries throughout the world, including Germany, Greece and Portugal, as well as the United States and Israel. In the Russian Far East women may be trafficked to China, Japan or Thailand.

Traffickers exploit people's desperation to escape the poverty which affects much of Russia. Organised criminal gangs take advantage of the lack of possibilities for legal migration. They operate through false employment agencies offering 'good jobs' abroad as waitresses, dancers, nurses, au pairs or labourers. The salaries promised are well above what they can hope to earn in Russia, and in many cases the agency arranges their transport and visas.

The reality is very different. On arrival their papers are taken away. Women are forced to work in brothels as prostitutes and are controlled through psychological coercion and physical violence, including beatings and rape. Men are forced to work long hours for little or no pay on construction sites or farms. Traffickers also force their victims to repay the cost of transportation, thus controlling them through a system of debt bondage. Debts can be as high as $30,000.

CASE STUDY: SERGEY'S STORY

When Sergey was 27 years old, he saw an advert in a local Russian newspaper for construction workers to go to Spain. The salary offered was $1,200 per month. This was more than ten times what he earned in his home town of Perm. He applied to the agency, which booked his plane ticket to Madrid on the condition that he would pay back the money when he started work.

On arrival in Spain, Sergey was picked up by a person from the 'agency' who took his passport. He was taken to Portugal and forced to work on a construction site without pay for several months. The site was surrounded by barbed wire. Without his passport he was afraid that the Portugese authorities would arrest him. One day Sergey managed to escape and begged his way to Germany. Because he did not have a passport, the German authorities arrested him. He said the police beat him and took away what little money he had before deporting him to Russia.

Sergey was traumatised by his experience and suffered psychological problems after his return. He was unable to work for several months, but did not receive counselling or support to help him overcome his ordeal. His traffickers were never prosecuted.

Trafficking to the UAE

Over the last decade, children from countries such as Bangladesh, Pakistan, Sudan and Yemen have been trafficked and used as camel jockeys in the United Arab Emirates (UAE).

The use of children as jockeys in camel racing is extremely dangerous and can result in serious injury and even death. Some children are also abused by the traffickers and employers, for example by depriving them of food and beating them. The children's separation from their families and their transportation to a country where the people, culture and usually the language are completely unknown leaves them dependent on their employers and de facto forced labourers.

In July 2005, the government of the UAE recognised the seriousness of this problem and announced the introduction of a new law prohibiting the use of children under 18 as camel jockeys.

While this is a significant step forward, questions remain over whether this legislation will be implemented in practice. The UAE Ministry of Interior itself estimated that there were roughly 2,800 camel jockeys under 10 years of age in the UAE in May 2005 – this despite the fact that the use of children under 14 as camel jockeys has been prohibited in the UAE for decades. Given the government's failure to apply previous laws, it remains to be seen whether it will take the necessary measures to tackle the trafficking of camel jockeys to the UAE and ensure that the 2005 legislation is properly enforced.

CASE STUDY: IRSHAD'S STORY

Irshad was just four years old when he was abducted from his home in Bangladesh and taken to Dubai in the UAE, by a friend of his father. He was given to a 'master' to be trained as a camel jockey. Irshad was woken at 4.00 a.m. and taken to the race-track at dawn. He was tied to an eight-foot-tall camel, which could reach speeds of up to 64 kilometres per hour. Irshad says he was given very little food or water in order to keep his weight down. He was consequently highly malnourished and underweight. Irshad sustained several injuries while working as a camel jockey.

Irshad's parents searched for him and eventually his father tracked him down in Dubai, but his visa expired and he was deported to Bangladesh without his son.

After three years as a camel jockey, Irshad was finally res-cued and repatriated by the Bangladeshi consulate with the help of the Bangladesh National Women Lawyers' Association (BNWLA), and reunited with his family.

Trafficking in the UK

In the UK there is a lack of statistical information on trafficking, but there is sufficient evidence to indicate that, at an absolute minimum, hundreds of people are being trafficked into the UK for sexual or labour exploitation each year.

Since 1995, West Sussex Social Services profiled more than 70 children who went missing from their care who they believed were victims of trafficking. Research by ECPAT UK in 2004 docu-mented 35 cases of child trafficking in 17 London boroughs, most of whom were trafficked for domestic work or prostitution. While many boroughs could not provide details of cases, 32 out of the 33 boroughs in London were concerned that they had a problem with trafficked children.

In relation to adults, the POPPY Project, which was set up to assist women trafficked into the UK for prostitution, dealt with

411 referrals between March 2003 and January 2005. Migrant workers are also subjected to threats, coercion and debt bondage in industries like agriculture, catering, building and domestic work. Research carried out by Anti-Slavery International in 2005–6 documented more than two dozen cases of individuals who were victims of trafficking for forced labour in the UK.

Trafficking for both sexual and labour exploitation became criminal offences in the UK in 2004. However, support and protection for trafficked people remains inadequate, with assistance only available to a limited number of women who are trafficked into prostitution and meet specified criteria for receiving support. There are no specialised services available to men, women or children trafficked into labour exploitation.

CASE STUDY: ELLEN'S STORY

When Ellen was 17, she was abducted by a group of men in Albania and taken to a flat where she was held for two months. During this time she was beaten and raped. Then a man came and made arrangements for them both to go abroad. At the time Ellen thought she had been rescued, but her new 'boyfriend' was another trafficker who took her to the UK, where he forced her into prostitution. She had to see between 15 and 40 customers a day and give the money to her trafficker. When she tried to refuse, she was beaten.

After about a year she was picked up in a police raid. She did not say anything to the police, because her trafficker had told her not to and she was afraid of getting her family into trouble. She was held at Heathrow airport for two days, while immigration officers arranged to have her sent back to Albania. No arrangements were made for her to be seen by an NGO in the UK or after she arrived back in Albania.

Ellen went back to live with her family, but received threatening phone calls in the early hours of the morning. Her family wanted her to go to the police, but Ellen did not trust the police in Albania. Concerned for herself and the safety of her family, she decided to let the traffickers take her back to the UK. A few months after she was trafficked to the UK for the second time, she managed to escape from her trafficker. She made an application to stay in the UK, but this was rejected by the Home Office.

Conclusion

States need to pass legislation that prohibits and punishes all forms of trafficking as set out in the United Nations Protocol to Prevent, Suppress and Punish Trafficking in Persons, Especially Women and Children. Approximately 90 states around the world, including the UAE and Indonesia, still have not done this.

It is also essential that trafficked people are provided with proper protection and support, in order to help them recover from their experiences and to ensure that they are protected from further human rights violations, including being re-trafficked. The only international standard which guarantees minimum standards of support and assistance to trafficked people is the Council of Europe Convention on Action Against Trafficking, but only 26 of the Council of Europe's 46 members had signed this convention at the time of writing. The UK and Russia are two of the states that have not committed themselves to implementing the convention.

Governments must also recognise that initiatives which only look at prosecution and protection issues will not be sufficient to counter the problem of trafficking in people. Policies must also be developed which aim to prevent trafficking by addressing the root causes of the problem.

One of the causes of trafficking is the growing inequality of wealth between and within countries. This is combining with an increasing, and often unacknowledged, demand for migrant workers in both developed and developing countries. These factors are fuelling migration. However, many governments have reacted to this by mounting campaigns that seek to evoke fear in potential migrants and dissuade them from travelling abroad, and by implementing more restrictive immigration policies.

This response is unlikely to deter migrants who are seeking work abroad as a means of survival. Furthermore, it has increased the profitability of trafficking by reducing regular routes for migration. Governments should promote regular and managed migration, as this can reduce trafficking by offering migrants a way of taking up jobs abroad which is safer, cheaper and allows them to better protect their human and labour rights in the country of destination.[1]

STATISTICS FROM **www.stopthetraffik.org**

- At least 12.3 million people are victims of forced labour worldwide. Of these, 2.4 million are as a result of human trafficking. ('A global alliance against forced labour', International Labour Organisation, 2005)
- 600,000–800,000 men, women and children are trafficked across international borders each year. Approximately 80 per cent are women and girls. Up to 50 per cent are minors. (US Department of State Trafficking in Persons Report, 2005)
- An estimated 1.2 million children are trafficked each year. (Child UNICEF UK trafficking Information Sheet, January 2003)
- The majority of trafficking victims arguably come from the poorest countries and poorest strata of the national population. ('A global alliance against forced labour', International Labour Organisation, 2005)
- Trafficking is the fastest-growing means by which people are caught in the trap of slavery. (Anti-Slavery International)
- Human trafficking is the third largest source of income for organised crime, exceeded only by arms and drug trafficking. (UN office on drugs and crime)

---

[1] For more information on trafficking and other contemporary forms of slavery, visit Anti-Slavery International's website at www.antislavery.org. To see publications which can be bought or downloaded free as PDFs, go to www.antislavery.org/homepage/resources/publication.htm.

HUMAN TRAFFICKING

- It is the fastest-growing form of international crime, already generating $7 billion per year in criminal proceedings. There are even reports that some trafficking groups are switching their cargo from drugs to human beings in search of high profits at lower risks. (UN office on drugs and crime)
- People are trafficked into prostitution, begging, forced labour, military service, domestic service, forced illegal adoption, forced marriage, etc.
- Types of recruitment include abduction, false agreement with parents, being sold by parents, travel with family, and orphans being sold from the street or institutions.

MIKE KAYE

Mike Kaye is communications manager at Anti-Slavery International. He has been working in the human rights field for more than 15 years and his previous jobs have included teaching in the University of Central America (Nicaragua); human rights fieldwork in El Salvador, Guatemala and Mexico; policy officer for the Central America Human Rights Committees; and parliamentary officer for the Refugee Council.

Anti-Slavery International was founded in 1839 by the same campaigners who led the campaign for the abolition of the slave trade in 1807 and is the oldest human rights organisation in the world. It remains the leading international organisation campaigning against slavery today.

If you want to help make slavery a thing of the past once and for all, then go to www.antislavery.org/2007 and add your name to the thousands of others who have already signed the declaration calling for measures to eradicate modern slavery and commemorate the end of the British slave trade. If you want to learn more about slavery, past and present, there is a range of publications which can be downloaded free as PDFs or bought online.

4: Investigating modern sex slavery

Father Shay Cullen, Preda Foundation

People as commodities

Slavery today is the same as it always was – a human person reduced to a commodity, deprived of freedom, working for nothing, exploited for profit, owned like an animal, forced to grovel and serve another, without pay or recompense. Worst of all, it is the exploitation of children in the organised sex industry – a billion-dollar business that runs on treachery and tyranny.

Child sex slaves are chained to beds, abused daily, threatened and tortured, punched and punished, beaten and bruised, and made a plaything for the powerful, a toy for the depraved. Many are murdered when no longer useful or a liability to the slave masters. Others commit suicide or perish from disease, abuse and despair.

The story of Maria, aged 13, a village girl, is all too common. She was taken from her impoverished parents for a pittance on the pretext of a job in Manila serving the rich. Instead, the sex traders and traffickers, the modern slavers, took her to Olongapo City, 130 kilometres north of Manila. There she was raped by her pimp.

Helpless and homeless, she was then sold nightly to the US Marines coming from the naval base on the shores of Subic Bay. In the 1970s and 80s I was mistaken for a marine many a time and invited to buy the sexual services of prostituted children. It was almost impossible to get any police co-operation. They were part of the dirty business, it seemed.

Frightened beyond belief with threats of mutilation and torture, Maria was locked in a small room behind the 'Body Shaft' sex club, near Magsaysay Drive, the notorious sex strip that was a haven for paedophiles and child abusers. There, five or six men forced themselves on her daily.

Preda makes a difference . . .

Maria and 18 other children were hospitalised with sexually transmitted diseases and I came to hear of it. Despite the cover-up by city officials and their efforts to have me deported, I exposed the terrible truth of this evil trade with the help of the Preda human rights team led by Alex Hermoso. Preda (People's Recovery, Empowerment, and Development Assistance Foundation) is an organisation I set up in 1974 to protect children from sexual exploitation and drug abuse.

We then began to campaign for the removal of the naval bases and the conversion of the facilities into factories, a project that would give work with dignity to the thousands of Filipinos enslaved in the sex business and working at the military base.

With the help of many groups, our campaign to remove the US bases succeeded in 1992 after a historic vote by the Philippine Senate. It was not the end of sex slavery. The international sex mafia returned a few years later and brought a new kind of global sex tourist.

. . . but the authorities stand idly by

Today, most of the customers are wealthy tourists from developed nations, preying on and exploiting the poor and the vulnerable. Slavery is still with us in an even more horrible and vicious manner, and the governments of rich nations are doing too little to investigate their criminals who come to places like the Philippines to enslave children and women; and so the criminals can operate the sex slave industry with impunity. The inaction of Western governments is seen by critics as permissive, as if to say, 'Better there than here.'

Child rapists and murderers Brett Tyler and Timothy Moss, both Britons, escaped to the Philippines after they kidnapped, raped and murdered nine-year-old Daniel Hanley from east London. They hid out in Olongapo, blending in with the resident community of foreign sex tourists and paedophiles. They brought young boys into their rented house on Waterdam Road, and abused them with the knowledge of local residents and officials. No one did anything. It was business as usual.

Moss returned to England and was arrested. British police sent out a request to locate the whereabouts of Tyler. Preda investigators mounted a search, found him in an isolated part of Olongapo City, and put the house under surveillance. I alerted the British police through the office of the Australian federal police in Manila, and Tyler was deported and received two life sentences in England. But many more remained undetected to continue trafficking and trading young innocent teenagers.

Moral collapse

This practice, and the impunity enjoyed by the child abusers, has eroded the spiritual and moral values of the Filipino family. Foreign influence and overbearing colonial superiority have weakened national dignity and pride. People have come to believe that 'white is right'. If the foreigners do it, then the practice of enslaving women and children for sexual gratification must be all right for everyone. Child abuse in the home and community has soared in recent years and only now is the full extent being uncovered.

There are an estimated 1.5 million sex tourists coming to Asia every year. Some powerful government officials, their relatives and friends, are business partners with the slick slavers who masquerade as tourist developers. Sex slavery, child pornography, cyber sex and child prostitution are all part of this evil commerce that has corrupted countless families and communities.

That's how it was for 13-year-old Anna Marie, a sex slave of her own father, who threatened to kill her and burn her brothers and sisters alive if she did not please his every sexual desire.

The spread of pornography through disks and cheap players has made the problem worse. One and a half million children, some as young as five and six years old, are captured, abducted and tortured to satisfy the fantasies and twisted sexual desires of these perverted human beings.

Modern slavery thrives because of incompetent courts, corrupted prosecutors, abusive police and a public that does not know or does not want to know about the human degradation of these innocent people. I have seen many paedophiles and slave masters walk free from useless courtrooms and porous prisons. In the Philippines no more than two traffickers have been convicted under the new law in the past three years. Undercover workers have been openly offered minors for sex for as little as £20. The sex traders are well protected and have no fear of the law or its enforcers.

Dedicated child defenders and agencies have waged campaigns – sometimes successfully – to stop the exploitation and abuse. They have confronted politicians and prosecutors, judges and juries, and social welfare offices, appealing for them to end the slavery, convict the criminals, cut loose the chains of the officers so they can get out of their offices and into the streets and sex dens to free the children – but they would not.

Prison nightmare

Then there is another kind of slavery, within the prison system. There was Jamie, twelve years old, a diminutive little boy, jailed with the rapists and murderers of Metro Manila. He was frail, skinny and very frightened when I found him shivering in a dark corner of an overcrowded cell, crammed with half-naked, sweating criminals. He was but one of thousands of children who are behind bars in the Philippines, not yet released despite a new law to end the jailing of children.

Jamie's 'crime' was playing cards on a street corner after school. The police said it was gambling, the family said it was child's play. The prosecutor never saw him and the judge never heard him. He was forgotten because the family could not afford to pay the bribe to have him released, and did not dare to challenge the power of the authorities.

The family brought him food just once a week. They had to pay the warden to get in. Jamie needed more than the daily handful of jail rice and spoonful of vegetables. It left him weak and hungry. Tuberculosis was floating, he was sucking it in on every breath – it was only a matter of time. Scabies spread like a bush fire, sores broke out all over his body and brought an agonising itch. AIDS was an ever-present danger.

He could have been anybody – your son, my student, a nephew, a grandson, a child of the world, even Jesus Christ, but nevertheless, behind bars, he was alone against the world, defeated, vulnerable and powerless.

Jamie was dragged into the toilet at night and repeatedly raped. Crying with the pain, he was beaten to shut up. He washed the adult prisoners' clothes so they would not beat him. He massaged their backs and sex organs so they would feed him. He cleaned the excrement-filled toilet and they would give him a space to lie down. It was survival; they made him a girlie-boy. It was the Philippine gulag for him, and as many as 20,000 more, all over the country.

He scratched the itch of the scabies and the mosquito bites until he bled, and the wounds became infected. There was no doctor or nurse, no medical treatment. He could not get out into the yard for the sun and the light. He became pale and his eyes sank into his head as if retreating from the evil of the world. He cried when the cockroach bit him, cried with the hunger and the fear and the loneliness. He prayed for his family to come, prayed for someone to save him, but no one came. He never had a chance of freedom from this dehumanising servitude. The nauseating smell of urine in the oven-baked air, the dank humidity, brought him to despair.

I found him shivering with a fever from the infection and naked but for tattered cotton shorts.

I demanded to know from the authorities the gravity of his crime, the length of his sentence, the weight of evidence. There was none, not a shred of paper where his name was typed, his case number shown, his existence recognised. There was no record of his detention because, according to the police and the warden and the guards, it never happened. There was no conviction, no punishment, and no unlawful arbitrary detention.

Jamie never existed on official records, like the disappeared, the abducted. He was a non-person to them. His imprisonment was just a mistake, they told me. No one was to blame, so take him away and cause us no trouble, they said.

The gate clanged open and Jamie was pushed out, petrified and shocked. He was in a daze and could not understand that the misery was over, the torture had ended; he was a slave no more. He boarded the van and was soon on the way to our Preda children's home, where hundreds of rescued children have recovered. Jamie recovered, despite the traumatic experience, but his childhood was stolen for ever. Eventually, we found his parents. They came and hugged and held each other and rejoiced.

Lives destroyed for profit

We humans must be the most depraved and corrupt species that ever walked the earth. No other creature enslaves as we do, for pleasure of power and profane profit. Humans capture, imprison and enslave all of creation, plants and animals, and their own kind too, and bend them to their will. Humans are the slavers of this world. No more wooden sailing ships ply the waves filled with sickened and prostrate Africans chained in their own vomit and waste, destined for the cottonfields of America or the plantations of Britain's territories. Their labour, sweat and tears filled the coffers of the traders in Liverpool and Boston, and the banks of London and New York. Now, the slavers are the traffickers and sex tourists travelling in style across oceans and continents to ravish the weak, who have been born into poverty and live in chains of debt.

The story of Jean and Mia

Jean and Mia were twins, born of a father they never knew, raised by a mother who did not care, who sold them off to a pimp when they were only 14 years old. They were raped in a sex bar the following week. I heard about their abduction and started an investigation.

It was a large, glittering façade that greeted me as I went inside looking for the teenagers. I had received a tip-off and was sure they were here. In the foyer a man dressed in black and bedecked with gold chains and sparkling diamond rings was the trafficker and slaver of children. He looked the part.

I was greeted as a potential customer with smiles and laughter. 'Have a good time, Joe!' the mamasan gushed and ushered me in.

Inside the club, the girls paraded as they were taught. They looked sad and sultry, caged and cringing, behind the make-up and the mascara. This was the modern-day auction. No more the wharfside platform lined with disembarked wrecks of suffering slaves cringing beneath the blows and whips of the slave seller. Now we had soft lights and music, and the even softer sell.

The trafficking of children and women is growing. I discovered Filipino children as young as 9–16 turned into child prostitutes in the back streets and bars of Angeles and Olongapo, Manila and Bulacan, Malinta and Cebu. They are trafficked to Japan, Korea, South Africa, Asia and the Middle East. Countries like the Philippines have a low rate of HIV/AIDS and so women and minors from these places are much in demand. That is why many sex tourists prefer the Philippines above other sex industry destinations.

There is no need nowadays for the slave hunters to storm the villages with musket, cutlass, rope and net. The recruiters and traffickers lure the youth with payments and promises of good jobs, but they end up prisoners of exploitation and abuse. Even jobs abroad are dangled before parents and cash payments and promises seal the deal – and the life of a village girl is damaged and destroyed, the hope of an education gone, a childhood stolen, dreams crushed.

I found neither Jean nor Mia that night, but picked up another tip that they were going to be sent abroad. Before that could happen, Jean had had enough abuse and slipped away and went back to her mother, who was part of the deal. She did nothing to rescue Mia, who was slated to be shipped out and sold off in Japan, where about 35,000 Filipino women and minors are trafficked into the 'entertainment' industry every year. Pressure is mounting on the Japanese to crack down on this trafficking that masquerades as 'visiting entertainers'.

I found Jean back in Olongapo and she told me where her sister was being held. I brought Preda's social workers, her mother and the police to the den, and we found 20 young women there. Several appeared to be teenagers, and Jean's sister Mia was among the captives.

Soon two pimps showed up with a man and a woman. The man was the same one in black and gold chains whom I had seen in the sex club. He was furious. The woman was shouting abuse at the police. It was tense and dangerous and I thought the man would pull out a gun. He demanded that the police should radio for their superiors. It was clear that he had paid off someone. The police I had with me were from another unit. They stayed outside, showing no interest in beginning an investigation. Instead they began to discuss what looked like a pay-off.

I went into the house, and saw and photographed a list of names and flights to Japan. Then I got Mia out of the house and into the van and we drove off. I only wish I could have rescued the others.

Back at the Preda home, both teenagers settled in quickly. During the emotional expression therapy, they cried and screamed, pouring out all their anger and hurt at their mother for selling them, at the abuser for raping them, crying out, 'Why did it happen?' They relived the abuse, but this time they had the confidence to open up. Their long-buried pain came pouring out and they were into the healing process. Eventually they recovered. But it was dangerous, as the traffickers had threatened to shoot their mother if they filed charges. Today, both sisters are enrolled in junior college.

Servant or slave?

Domestic servants brought from the countryside are imprisoned in the houses and apartments of the rich and are virtual slaves too. They are like sex toys, shared at night among the male members of the family. They are passed from bedroom to bedroom, basement to attic, raped repeatedly. Some are brought to parties in swanky hotels and given as a gift for the night to a business partner to close a deal, appease a crony or seal a contract.

They are under the psychological whip of the master. They are trained to be docile and submissive, obedient and grateful. The training uses intimidation and threats. 'Your family will starve, your brothers will be arrested, your parents will be shot,' they are told.

Alice, 15, was bought from her village in Negros Island and used as a domestic servant for a wealthy family in Alabang, South Manila. She was made a sex slave, and passed around young men and abused. When I was asked to help, we contacted the local Social Welfare office and asked for her birth certificate so that we would have evidence to charge the abusers. Inexplicably, the government workers talked to the recruiter, not the parents, in that village, and in a few days the child was released. No effort was made to bring the traffickers or the abusers to justice. It was another dirty deal.

It is common practice for officials at district level to settle trafficking and rape cases by arranging a compensation payment to the parents.

Talk is not enough

Cherry Kingsley was only a naive and curious teenager when she was trapped and controlled by a sex ring in Canada and sold for sex as a prostituted child. Now 30 years old, she told an international conference recently of her ordeal and how she had seen her friends and other children beaten and bruised, tortured and killed, by the sex mafia. It is not only in the underdeveloped world that youth are exploited by the sex slave gangs. Their lives are cut short by a painful death from AIDS-related diseases, drugs, alcohol or suicide. Cherry told the delegates that outrage was not enough. Talk is important, but practical solutions are absolutely necessary.

Sex slavery in Britain

Operation Pentameter in Britain has brought together all police forces into a co-operative effort to get an understanding of sex slavery in Britain. They discovered the tip of the iceberg when investigations uncovered trafficking rings bringing thousands of women and children annually into Britain.

They learned that teenagers as young as 15 were trafficked and auctioned off in the coffee shops at Stansted airport, then the wholesaler sold them to brothel owners in the Midlands and elsewhere. These are East European youth desperate for jobs: to escape from the drudgery of rural life with no future, they will take any offer.

Like Trudy, who was a teenager, aged 15, when her parents in Eastern Europe were offered money to allow her to go to London to sell ice cream. She was sold by the child trafficker at the airport to a brothel owner who raped her, locked her in a room, and forced her to have several men a day. Then Trudy was sold to a rich client who turned her into a trophy girl to impress his friends. During a party this brave girl escaped. She ran for an hour until she found someone who would listen to her story and help her. She was able to testify and many traffickers were caught and convicted.

Impunity and ignorance

In developing countries, family dynasties control the government and political parties are fronts for feuding families battling for their corporate interests. Their family members or relatives are appointed to sensitive posts in the important government departments. In effect, the rich and powerful are so corrupt that they are above the law and are protected from prosecution and accountability. This impunity is an open door to slavery, trafficking of minors, sex tourism and child labour. It is the rich who own and operate the brothels, hotels, sex bars and resorts in concert with foreign investors. They invite the tourists and pander to their every need, and allow the delivery of women and children to their hotel or beach chalet.

The culture of impunity of the rich and powerful encourages corruption and depravity down the chain of command, infecting the whole system.

Even the United Nations refugee camps have faced scandals as refugees endure unpaid labour, exchange sexual favours for food, and suffer incarceration without hearings for trivial offences. In response, Secretary General Kofi Annan declared a zero tolerance for such sexual abuses and human rights violations. But zero tolerance has been met with zero prosecutions.

That is why slavery continues to this day. The powerful lord it over the weak and the vulnerable. The wretched of the earth are in their control and under their whip and they can do what they want with them.

In the West, sophisticated societies feign ignorance, prefer apathy before the truth, and hypocrisy abounds. These predominantly consumer societies treat people as consumables, so trafficking of people thrives. They forget that their nation's economy and the welfare benefits it delivers to them these days derived from international trade that ran on slave labour.

In Asia, Africa and parts of South America, billion-dollar industries benefit from child labour and exploited workers. Free trade, the weakening of the labour unions and the migration of the educated and skilled workers leave a predominantly agricultural-based economy. In the overpopulated developing world, that is a recipe for exploitation and abuse. A paternalistic, feudalistic society dominated by landlords and warlords operates behind a semblance of democracy in many of these countries.

Powerlessness and ignorance allow such a system to exist and continue with impunity. Its principle features are the lack of accountability and absence of meaningful law that protects the rights of the most vulnerable and places justice within the reach of the poor.

Children in danger

In the Philippines, a working child is found in every three homes, and the youngest can be only five years old. They work on farms and small plantations, they plant the sugar, they cut the corn, they harvest the rice, carry the water, gather the bananas, spread the chemicals, spray the pesticide and suffer disease, fatigue and a life of sorrow without end. Strong laws ban such forms of slavery, but they are rarely implemented. In the sex industry they are almost totally ignored.

In the cities, the child workers gather scraps, scratch the garbage dumps, beg on the streets, work in the brothels and backstreet factories and bakeries. There is no end to it. In the Philippines, 4 million of the 25 million children are working for little or no pay and are not in school.

What can we do?

This can be changed only by a concerted international political will to do so. The International Criminal Court must extend its jurisdiction to cover crimes involving organised sex trafficking, the enslavement of children and any systematic violation of their human rights. Yet campaigns are of limited use if there is no moral or spiritual values system to stand and fight for, if there are too few people with convictions who can be empowered and mobilised for social movements and political action.

Awareness building, convincing and converting people to have a heart for all the victims is the challenge for anti-slavery advocates. More people have to be persuaded to take a stand for the dignity of every child, every woman, every enslaved person. They can join a rally, form an action group, share their wealth, lend their name to a petition, do something worthwhile with their lives and property, to rattle the gates of parliament, to work to change the world.

Instead of the Riviera, Spain or Brighton, people ought to visit the developing world and meet and be inspired by the good and selfless people who live out their faith, who meet their God in liberating people from every kind of slavery and oppression. Here, among the poor and the needy, they can participate in a great movement of compassion and caring.

There are countless dedicated people working to change the global injustice, giving education and enlightenment to the illiterate and the outcasts, and empowering women and children to seek justice. They work selflessly to liberate the enslaved, lift up the captives, throw open the prison cells, close down the brothels with legal battles, and release the children and women. They bring a new life of dignity and respect to those so cruelly abused, abandoned and enslaved. There is no greater joy than to know you have given your all, done your best, and shared your heart and your wealth with those who deserve it most.

What did Jesus do?

No true Christian can turn away and do nothing in the face of the reality of modern slavery. Jesus Christ brought to the consciousness of the world the sacred dignity and rights of every human being, irrespective of social status. By words and actions, Jesus made it clear that the poor, the abandoned, the sick, the wounded, the prostituted women and abused children, the beggars, even the criminals hanging on the cross, all the enslaved, share equally God's love and redemption.

He challenged us all by giving away the kingdom of heaven to the poor whom he blessed. They who had less deserved more, because human greed made them suffer greatly, he said. Lazarus dying at the gate of Dives' palace had only the dogs to lick his wounds and show compassion. The selfish rich share so little, not even crumbs.

Jesus is not only one with them, but mysteriously he is in them. What you do to them, you do to me, he said. His real presence is found in them, you might say, and we can meet him there and be one with God, infinite goodness. If we truly love God, we love the poor and the oppressed, and that means we take their side, wash their feet, lift them up, and give them a place at the Lord's table, so they can have their fill of justice for which they hunger and thirst so much. It is not enough for Christians to give the crumbs and pitiful handouts of discarded clothing and spare change. We have to change the world and renew it in God's image and likeness.

The irresponsible rich; owners of sweatshops, oppressive underpaying employers, brothel operators, traffickers and modern gang masters – all are slave owners who make fortunes by exploitation of the poor and the vulnerable. They are invited to repent and believe in Jesus and make amends. Like Zacchaeus, they can repay fourfold all that they took from their victims.

We are all challenged to get beyond churchgoing as the measure of faith and the path to redemption. Jesus asks more: he wants our unselfish love to be given to him through serving the poor. When we say we love God, are we giving without counting the cost or asking for rewards? True Christianity is imitating Jesus, following his example, taking the risks as he did, enduring rejection and hardship, injustice and abuse. For him, the wretched of the earth are the precious people of God. We must lift up the downtrodden, free the captives and give freedom to the children, and cure the spiritual blindness and loneliness of the rich with the experience of friendship with Jesus Christ,

SHAY CULLEN

Shay Cullen, an Irish Columban missionary, went to the Philippines in 1969 and discovered the abuse of thousands of women and children, some as young as nine years old, exploited and enslaved in a sex industry that catered to the US military and international sex tourists. Swarms of hungry and abandoned children roamed the streets, many on drugs, some sold as sex slaves. Others only six years old were behind bars. Thousands of child workers suffered abuse, disease and neglect. Father Shay set out to free the children and women from these dehumanising and slave-like conditions and founded the People's Recovery, Empowerment, and Development Assistance (Preda) Foundation to save them. Preda is an internationally known organisation and Father Shay has received three nominations for the Nobel Peace Prize in the recent past. For more information, see preda@info.com.ph.

Keep up to date with Father Shay's initiatives to promote and protect the dignity and the human rights of the Filipino people, especially of women and children, at www.preda.org.

At www.preda.net you can learn about Preda's important fair-trade work, which addresses the issues of poverty and strives to provide alternative livelihoods to the rural poor to help them prosper and live a life of dignity in their village homes.

Father Shay's inspiring autobiography *Passion and Pain* exposes the extent of the trafficking and abuse of children for customers of sex tourism from rich countries of every nationality – the worst kind of modern slavery. It tells the powerful story of the brave and dedicated Filipinos fighting this evil and how they restore the hope and dignity of the children and give them a new start in life. *Passion and Pain* was published in 2006 by Killynon House Books, Mullingar, Ireland.

5: India's Dalits: Modern slavery's biggest challenge

Dr Joseph D'Souza, Dalit Freedom Network, Operation Mobilisation

The institution of caste is a system at war with truth and nature.
William Wilberforce

Manjula is a modern slave.[1] From the age of four, this child accompanied her mother at 5 o'clock every morning to the matchstick production factory in Sivakasi, Tamil Nadu, India. Forsaking sleep, forsaking safety, she and her mother worked in hazardous, disgusting conditions, for just a few rupees a day. They watched every month as dozens of their 'colleagues' received chemical burns and terrible injuries from explosions. They lived in fear of the work environment and of physical abuse if they did not meet their production quota for the day.

Today, Manjula is twelve years old. Sadly, her younger sister, Kavitha, has also taken up the matchstick trade. Her parents live in a never-ending cycle of debt.

---

[1] These are true stories, but the names have been changed.

Manjula and Kavitha are the collateral with which those debts will be repaid. With scars on their frail, undernourished bodies to tell the tale, these girls have been denied a childhood; denied a life of freedom. What hope do they have for a better tomorrow?

Premila is also a modern slave. It was her eighteenth birthday in her small village in rural Bihar. Her parents, desperate to escape their impoverished plight, signed their daughter over to a nightmare. For the paltry sum of 800 rupees ($18), she was sold to a man living in faraway Punjab state. He claimed there were no 'good women' in his village and therefore he was forced to buy a wife. 'Wife' is a loose term. 'Sexual slave' would be more accurate.

For one or two years Premila was used as a modern-day concubine. There was no marriage ceremony. There was no hope of marital love in her future. Her body was used and abused at the will of this man, her 'husband', and of any of his male relatives who came to call. It was a living hell. But her days were about to get worse.

Eventually, a new investment opportunity presented itself and Premila was turned out of her new 'family' in Punjab and sold to a well-known prostitution ring in the nation's capital, New Delhi.

The sex trafficking trade runs rampant and Premila brought a relatively good price: 5,000 rupees ($109). She joined thousands of other women who exist in impoverished, disease-ridden, dangerous conditions. She was forced to sell or give her body under threat of abuse or death. What else could she do?

Premila was a 'good' employee and was traded yet again to the streets of Mumbai for 35,000 rupees ($762). It was here that she was finally rescued. Returned to her home town in Bihar, however, she was a broken woman. She will never marry. She will likely die young – used, abused and forgotten.

An unbelievable reality

Manjula and Premila are just two of millions of oppressed children and women living as virtual slaves in India. Slaves to the upper caste; slaves to men; slaves to all society. They have no hope of rescue or of ever being truly free.

Manjula and Premila are slaves and the world stands by, simply watching.

Yes, global awareness and outrage over the issues of child labour and trafficking of persons are on the rise. The International Labour Organisation (ILO) seeks to eliminate the worst forms of child labour by 2016. The US State Department has put India on its Tier 2 Watch List of human trafficking, stating their desire to secure freedom for the exploited. The United Nations (UN) global human trafficking report acknowledges that India has failed to show evidence of efforts to address this atrocity. Church groups and NGOs pay the debts held against bonded child labourers to set them free.

Are these global efforts enough? No. Despite this, child labour in India is still on the rise. Statistics from the Indian government-appointed Commission on Labour Standards and International Trade in 1995 show that child labour in India is increasing by at least 4 per cent annually. It appears that global outrage is not enough.

An incomprehensible fate

The extent of the problem of bonded child labour and human trafficking is staggering.

There are an estimated 40–115 million child labourers in India today, 15 million of whom are in debt bondage or modern slavery. These children work under conditions of servitude to repay the debts of their parents, grandparents, relatives or guardians. Industries employing bonded child labourers include silk production, carpet weaving, beedi (cigarette) rolling, silver fabrication, gemstone polishing, leather production, brick making, rice milling, restaurant/tea shop service, truck stop cleaning, domestic work and prostitution. Employer-induced beatings are frequent and violent. Working conditions are inhumane and promote disease.

Millions of girls and women are trafficked for prostitution and slave labour – both interstate within India, and in the neighbouring countries of Pakistan, Bangladesh and Nepal. The atrocity reaches hundreds of thousands of minor and teenage Tribal girls who work in affluent urbanised areas, with about 50,000 in New Delhi, India's capital. There is no enforceable legal consequence to protect such young girls and women and their status in society traps them in a less than honourable reputation. Sexually transmitted diseases abound, but they have no money for treatment. They are resigned to a life of physical and sexual exploitation, a life worse than death.

The vast majority of these bonded child labourers and girls and women trafficked in India are 'Dalits'.

The ignoble caste system

One cannot understand India without comprehending the discriminating and oppressing ideology of the caste system in Indian life. Caste dominates people's lives from birth to death, divides and grades society into impenetrable levels of human worth based on birth and heritage. It controls and regulates India's social, economic, political and religious life.

The Dalits (meaning 'broken' or 'crushed') make up the Scheduled Castes and Scheduled Tribes, and number about 250 million people. 'Scheduled' means they are listed in a special 'index' appended to the constitution. They were known as the 'Untouchables' because they were deemed literally untouchable by the upper castes. The Scheduled Tribes were defined as 'Criminal Tribes' because they occasionally challenged, with arms, the dominance of the local landlords.

'Backward Castes', about 40 per cent of the population, are known as the Sudras, or the slave 'vassal' caste. They are above the Dalits, but still socially and economically depressed. The Dalits, Backward Castes and Low Castes comprise nearly 70 per cent of India's population.

Caste discrimination is 'India's silent apartheid' of 3,000 years, although Dalit leader Udit Raj states, 'Caste is worse than apartheid.' The caste system is an ideologically sanctioned racism that has maimed, dehumanised and destroyed hundreds of millions of people through the ages, and continues today in the twenty-first century.

India is not a homogenous society where there is a level playing field on which everyone can prosper. Trafficked women and bonded labour children trapped in modern slavery are mainly Dalits and the answer will not come easily.

Tackling an unsolvable problem

So what is the solution to this growing problem?

The way of legislation

Some want stricter legislation, but both practices – child labour and human trafficking – are illegal according to Indian law. Protective legislation does exist in several forms (i.e., the Child Labour (Prohibition and Regulation) Act, 1986; and Articles 14, 21, 23 and 24 of the Indian constitution). However, the political will and ability to enforce this legislation is nowhere to be found. Corruption, indifference and simple economics prevent those in power from consistently prosecuting the perpetrators, and criminal justice has failed the poor, the disempowered and the oppressed. Fewer than 2 per cent of cases that are registered as crimes against Dalits ever reach conviction.

Recently, a Dalit woman activist from Bihar was refused a passport to attend a UN conference on discrimination against women, and this decision was overturned only after an uproar in the Bihar state legislative assembly. Such cases of blatant discrimination abound.

The way of intervention

The *Asian Age* newspaper in May 2006 told the story of over 30 young boys who had been kidnapped from Bihar and taken to Karnataka, to work in conditions which denied them food, clothing and sunlight. The state government revelled in rescuing these young victims, promising to rehabilitate the boys, refusing to send them home until assured of proper treatment in the future.

Some groups pay the debts of children in bondage, allowing them to attend school. Others establish homes for girls caught in the sex trade, exposing the middlemen and traffickers.

Nonetheless, India's modern slavery must be addressed at the root – the community-based conditions which create the exploitation of children, girls and oppressed adults.

The way of international boycott

The solution does not lie in international sanctions or banning exports produced by child labour. Boycotts do not reach the heart of these desperate problems.

This is a domestic problem, with only 8 per cent of India's child labour force engaged in making exportable goods. The rest are consumed within India itself.

Another solution may seem to be international assurance of adequate wages or remuneration through multinational companies (i.e. outsourcing, information technology, accounting, customer service, manufacturing, etc.). The theory is that this would ease pressure on women and children to contribute to the family income through 'regular' child labour, prostitution or debt bondage.

The problem is that such Dalit groups do not speak English, do not have a globalised education, and do not have the necessary skills to be hired by a multinational company.

The Musahars – a dark blot on human civilisation

Outside intervention will surely never help over two million 'Musahars' of Uttar Pradesh and Bihar. This people group – called the Dalits of the Dalits – face extreme destitution and isolation known to no other person on earth. The word 'Musahar' literally means 'rat-eater' and clearly identifies the state of their existence. They suffer economically, medically, psychologically, socially and politically more than any other group within India. Strict religious and social guidelines dictate every aspect of their lives. There are rules on the location and type of housing, employment, working conditions, marriage and even burial – all designed to protect the upper caste from being contaminated by Musahar blood.

Naturally, those suffering the worst are the women in Musahar society. They are considered worthless, sexually and physically exploited by the upper castes.

Mudra Rakhsas, an eminent writer and activist of the Dalits and Backward Castes, recently asked Musahar children what they wanted to be when they grew up. The children replied in unison, 'Nothing.' They meant it because there was no future for them in 'India Incorporated', as *Time* magazine recently described India.

This problem cannot be solved by intervention. It must start with a deep transformation from within society.

The answer: make Dalit freedom a global campaign

There is an underlying assumption that a certain portion of mankind is of lesser value than the rest. This worldview thinks that these inferior human beings are destined by fate and the gods to serve others in virtual slavery. Such a mindset affects both the oppressed and the oppressor within the caste system, and condemns millions of children and women on a generational basis.

This worldview based on the caste ideology results in dire poverty for oppressed Dalits. A burden of debt and a lack of land, education and modern opportunity, among other factors, make their existence a virtual hell on earth.

The world should rejoice in William Wilberforce's (and others') outstanding work for humanity, while at the same time weeping with the millions of female sex workers and millions more bonded child labourers.

There is truly only one answer to the modern slavery experienced by women, children and oppressed peoples in India: we must make Dalit freedom a global campaign.

It is time for champions of the Dalit Freedom Movement to emerge around the world at this critical time in history to lead this all-important campaign. There are already significant Dalit leaders in India who want to change their world.

The slave trade and apartheid collapsed after global outrage. The same is true for India today. Those who perpetuate and derive profit from the caste system and the exploitation of Dalits will not relinquish what has become a lucrative way of growing strong economically and politically, unless strong global social pressure is raised against the practice. Only then will we ever see the end to modern-day slavery in India.

Dalits are found in South Asia, Africa, the UK, the US, Canada, Surinam and a host of other nations. Discrimination by the upper castes even in foreign lands continues. Investigate whether Dalits have become priests in temples outside India. Try to discover how many Dalit priests exist overseas. You will find none.

The Dalit problem is a global problem and a solution can only come when the whole world rallies around this issue.

Transformation begins with education

Beyond the global campaign for Dalit Freedom, education is an important key.

We must find a way to get children – especially girls – into school. They must gain knowledge and skills that will help them vocationally in the future. This schooling need not be traditional, and increased enforcement of laws to keep children in school may not be effective. An acceptance of the value of education must be fostered in every city, town, village and small community around the nation. Parents must be willing to sacrifice economically and socially today to see the long-term benefits of education in the generation to come.

The bottom line?

India's young must be in school in an atmosphere that promotes the values of education, learning skills, personal worth and human dignity within their entire community. Child labour and human trafficking must be eradicated.

Breaking the cycle of poverty is not easy. This is no secret. In fact, the battle against poverty is high on the global agenda today. There are concerts. There are campaigns. There are conventions. There are protests. However, awareness and fundraising are not the answer.

A true end to global poverty must address the root issues that cause poverty. Child labour and human trafficking perpetuate poverty, and this must be addressed before poverty will end. Child labourers and female sex workers mature into adults who lack the skills and, often, the physical abilities which would qualify them to work in any industry, thereby forcing the children of the future to adopt the same plight that modern-day adults have faced for decades.

Education is a major answer.

Further, this education must be a 'globalised' education with English included from day one. This is so important, because 'India Incorporated' – part of the new economy and new technology – is largely driven by an English education, which is not accessible to the oppressed minority.

The Dalit Freedom Movement is fully committed to providing this type of education to free children from potential slavery.

The key to success is the full partnership by Dalit leaders and women around the nation. In every location in which schools are placed, the local leadership of the community needs to support and implement an educational strategy.

The schools must operate with basic structures (building, classrooms, uniforms, qualified teachers, meals and books) and cater to mainly Dalit children – both girls and boys – who need to receive a quality dual-language (English and local language) education in a loving, productive environment in which students of all religions, castes and genders can flourish equally.

We cannot build third-class schools for 'third-class people ' – i.e. the Dalits, Tribals and other oppressed caste groups. Equality must be our primary value.

Practical help for today

Beyond education for Dalit children, the Dalit Freedom Movement is committed to furthering economic development among today's generation of Dalit adults. We want to see the Dalits learn financial management skills through 'self-help groups' which teach fiscal security through savings, local accountability, community generation of funding and positive repayment of loans. We are committed to training men and women in marketable skills such as tailoring, driving, computer use, bicycle repair and ironing. We want to see Dalit people make financial investment in agriculture and restoration of land. We want to produce macro-enterprise opportunities for Dalits with newly gained skills.

We believe that the end to slavery and poverty begins at a local level with skills training and local generation of funds. Economic development helps today's Dalit adults focus on a better tomorrow. It allows their children to go to school and avoid debt bondage. It allows Dalit women to contribute to the family through legitimate means and not through the sale of their womanhood.

Global challenge

We believe in the truths of human equality, freedom of conscience and equal opportunity for all. We reject all forms of racism, caste discrimination, colour prejudice and gender discrimination. We invite all concerned people everywhere to adopt this same attitude. This is a movement which requires a multitude of people from around the world. None of us can make a lasting impact alone.

This is your chance to become aware. This is your chance to act. Please join us and become part of the struggle for the emancipation of Dalits and the freedom of women and bonded child labourers everywhere.

DR JOSEPH D'SOUZA

Dr Joseph D'Souza leads multiple organisations both in India and internationally. He is the international president of the Dalit Freedom Network, whose mission is to empower the Dalits in their quest for human dignity, economic development and socio-spiritual freedom. Dr D'Souza is an activist for social justice and freedom of conscience and works for the cause of the marginalised and oppressed in different parts of the world. He is also the associate international director of Operation Mobilisation. In India he serves as the president of the All India Christian Council.

For more information on how you can join the fight against slavery in India, please contact the Dalit Freedom Network at info@dalitnetwork.org. Joseph D'Souza would be delighted to receive your e-mails at joseph@josephdsouza.com. Visit www.dalitnetwork.org and www.josephdsouza.com.

6: Chocolate slaves

Kate Blewett and Brian Woods, True Vision

Our journey into the world of slavery in the Ivory Coast was a deeply shocking and brutal one. It was something for which nothing could have prepared us.

A brutal story

Four days before we met him, Drissa's life of slavery came abruptly to an end. As he sat in the shade of a plane tree in the courtyard of the home of the Malian consul in Bouake, central Ivory Coast, Drissa knew he was lucky to be alive.

All of the 18 young men who had been rescued alongside Drissa had the same blank expressions. After up to five years as slaves harvesting cocoa that would be sold to make chocolate in Europe and the USA, Drissa and his friends were finding it hard to adapt to their new-found freedom.

For us, the greatest shock came when Drissa painfully, gingerly, took off his shirt. We made *The Dying Rooms* and filmed girl babies who had been deliberately left to starve to death; for *Innocents Lost* we filmed children in Greece who had been kept in cages for most of their short lives; in South America we saw the victims of police death squads. But thankfully we can both still be shocked by just how brutal one human being can be to another. Drissa's body was covered from head to foot in slowly healing wounds. Each one was originally a cut between one and two inches long. Some were healing neatly into thin, dark scars; others had become infected and billowed into angry, red, weeping sores. He had nearly died a slave.

Drissa had no idea how long he had been whipped for; the other boys said it was around half an hour. From their experience, it would take a year for Drissa to recover from the beating. For us, looking at this broken man, it seemed that he would perhaps never recover.

They told us that if the Malian consul had not come to rescue them, Drissa would almost certainly have died. Too many wounds had become infected, they said, and not enough maggots were feasting on the pus to keep the wounds clean.

Modern slaves

We had come to the Ivory Coast in search of modern slaves – defined as men, women and children who are paid nothing for their work, controlled by violence and unable to leave. But here we found young men who not only satisfied the modern definition, but also fitted the popular image of men who were bought and sold in an open market, locked up at night, and beaten viciously if they attempted to run away.

This had been Drissa's crime. After six months on the plantation he had decided he could no longer take the arduous work, the long hours and the threats of violence. The farmer who had bought him told his slaves that a spell had been cast over them, and that if they tried to escape they would be paralysed as soon as they crossed the threshold of the farm. Drissa decided to risk it. Coming from the dry savannah of Mali to the north of the Ivory Coast, he had never seen the dense jungle of the coast before. He had no idea where he was, and had no idea which way to run, but late one morning, run he did.

Drissa was free for just six hours, hopelessly lost in the thick forest. The farmer found him before the sun went down that day. He took him back to the compound and on the deep red earth, in front of the other 17 slaves, he started to beat him with a cane rod, demanding that Drissa explain how he had managed to overcome the spell. The other men were then ordered to carry Drissa into the shed that was their dormitory – the only building with a lock on the door. First thing the next morning, Drissa was dragged out and beaten again.

Rescue at last

Fortunately for Drissa, despite this very clear warning another boy tried to escape two months later, and this time succeeded. Victor managed to find a fellow Malian in a local village (previous escapees had not been so lucky – they were discovered by other farmers, and duly returned to their slave master). Victor was taken to Abdul Macko, the Malian consul in Bouake. The consul told us that Victor was so terrified of the slave master that he could not even bring himself to say his name. After several days Victor did finally describe how to get to the farm, although he would not return there himself. Going there with an armed guard, Consul Macko found 16 young men locked in a shed, and Drissa hidden in the forest – he had been left to die from his wounds. In Consul Macko's words, 'When we found them, they were unrecognisable as human beings, as if they came from another world.'

A journey of fear

The consul drew us a map, and the next day we drove off into the forest in search of the slave master.

The farm was about three hours' drive from the nearest proper road, more than a day's walk. As we stopped in villages to reconfirm directions, we were warned that we were crossing bandit country.

It was now that the fear really set in. In the middle of nowhere, Kate heard the words of the villager ringing inside her head: 'The bandits will kill you if you don't give them everything you have, or if you don't have what they want. They'll just kill you . . .'

The idea of life ending on this off-road mud track in the middle of cocoa plantation land left a deafening silence bouncing around inside the jeep.

We emerged from the thick forest of the valley into the surreal landscape of the ridge. Some time before, a forest fire, either caused by lightning or deliberately set to clear the land, had killed the trees that towered more than 150 feet over the track in the valley. Up here the charred trunks of the trees still stood erect, bereft of branches, skeletal, like giant black toothpicks. Around them the forest was trying to regain control, but nothing had yet grown more than a foot above the ground.

A few minutes later we arrived at the farm buildings where the young men had been enslaved. Nervous ourselves about the violence of which this man was capable, we moved forwards in an outwardly confident manner. Inside, the alarm bells were ringing. 'Are we doing the right thing? What if he's armed? What if there's more than one slave master here? What if . . .?'

An evasion of truth

The farmer, Yeo Djomon, was clearly shocked to see three white people arrive in a four-wheel-drive vehicle. We walked in with cameras slung over our shoulders and already running. We had no idea how friendly or hostile this man might be, and wanted to capture his reactions on camera whatever they might be.

In the event Yeo Djomon was cordial but defensive. Around him were half a dozen farm workers, mostly members of his extended family. They were dressed in ripped and ragged t-shirts and shorts, so filthy that they were all the same uniform red-brown colour. The farmer was dressed in jeans, a black-and-white plaid shirt and a bright red pullover, all very clean – a startling contrast.

We needed to be very careful about how we introduced ourselves through our questioning. We started with the economics of cocoa farming, and in common with all the other farmers we had spoken to, he told us that the all-time low price of cocoa was making it difficult to get by as a cocoa grower. He then went on to explain how he and other farmers bought their labourers at a market in Korhogo in the north of the Ivory Coast. Men and women called 'locateurs' would bring the young men down from Mali with false promises of well-paid work on the coast, then sell them to cocoa farmers. So, we asked, were the men free to leave whenever they liked? Yes, of course . . . Then he hesitated before adding, 'Except the younger ones, the ones who've been here for less than two years. We can't allow them to leave, because that would be a loss of investment for us.'

When we asked him about the beatings, he initially simply accused the boys of lying. But when we told him we had seen the wounds, he tried a new tack. The wounds we had seen, he said, were due to a lack of supervision: when left unattended they would fight amongst themselves . . .

A widespread horror

Is Yeo Djomon an unusually evil man? Perhaps. Or maybe he is just the product of his environment. As we travelled to other farms around the Ivory Coast, it became clear that although the beatings he meted out for attempted escapes were particularly brutal, the use of violence to control workers was accepted as part of everyday life. Dozens of boys we spoke to on farms all over the west of the Ivory Coast had not been paid for over a year, had been beaten by their farmers with fists, canes or whips, and were too afraid to run away.

One man we spoke to, Diaby Dembele, has worked in and around the cocoa farms for almost 20 years. He told us that if we had the time and resources to look, we would find some slaves on 90 per cent of Ivory Coast cocoa farms. Almost half the world's cocoa came from the Ivory Coast at the time, so if Diaby Dembele's estimate was correct, the hands of slaves touched almost half the world's chocolate.

The human price of chocolate

For us, the most abiding memory of the Ivory Coast will be the sight of Drissa's battered body. Sometimes when we film a scene of horror, the emotional impact of the scene becomes even more powerful in the course of the edit. As we compress what we experienced over an hour or more into just a few minutes of screen time, the sights and sounds become intensified. But somehow, in the case of Drissa, the process has worked the other way round: the camera has sanitised his wounds, made them two-dimensional, robbed them of their raw horror.

But perhaps even more shocking than the brutality suffered by Drissa is the fact that no one has ever told this story before. For 50 years the multinational confectionery and food companies have been buying their cocoa from the farmers of the Ivory Coast, and organisations like the World Bank have been saying they are doing everything possible to alleviate the suffering of the poor there. How is it possible that no one has ever before thought to visit the farms and speak to the workers, to discover just how many of them are not merely poor and exploited, but modern-day slaves in the most brutal sense?

For Drissa, the nightmare of slavery is over. He has now gone back to Mali with tales of slavery in the forest of the Ivory Coast that may discourage some of his friends from believing the promises of the locateurs.

We asked Victor, the man whose escape led to the rescue of his 17 fellow slaves, if any of them had ever tasted chocolate.

'No, we have never tasted chocolate.'

'Millions of people in Britain eat chocolate every day,' we told him. 'What would you say to them?'

'If I had to say something to them, it would not be nice words. They buy something that I suffer to make. They are eating my flesh.'

The enslavement of Drissa

Drissa's story is told in *Slavery – A Global Investigation* by True Vision's multi-awarding winning documentary makers Kate Blewett and Brian Woods. The utterly devastating film focuses on three separate industries where slaves are still to be found: the cocoa industry in the Ivory Coast, domestic slavery in Britain and the USA, and the carpet industry in northern India. This film isn't all bad news, however. The film-makers also look at how slavery can be fought, both here and abroad, without making the poor poorer. Kate and Brian say, 'We made *Slavery – A Global Investigation* because we wanted to make a difference.'

KATE BLEWETT AND BRIAN WOODS

Kate Blewett and Brian Woods are two of the UK's most award-winning documentary makers. The first time they worked together they made *The Dying Rooms*, in 1997, which went on to win over 20 international awards, including the Prix Italia and Peabody, as well as changing China's policy on state orphanages. It became Channel Four's best-selling single documentary and has been screened in over 60 countries.

Since then a series of campaigning international documentaries has garnered seven Emmies, four BAFTA nominations, two Peabodies and around 40 other international awards. Exposing slavery on the cocoa plantations of West Africa led to the industry adopting the first ever industry-wide anti-slavery protocol; *The Real Sex Traffic* is now being used by the US State Department and UK police to train officers in the sensitive handling of women trafficked for the sex trade; *Dying for Drugs* is being used in a court case in the US against Pfizer; *Eyes of a Child* affected British government policy on child poverty. The BAFTA-winning *Orphans of Nkandla*, which Brian made with his wife Deborah, led directly to over £2 million being donated to projects supporting orphaned and vulnerable children in South Africa.

Keep up to date with their great films at www.truevisiontv.com.

7: If shirts could only speak, if we would only listen

Dame Anita Roddick, Founder, The Body Shop

I returned recently from Bangladesh, and I am angry. Not, of course, with the people. They were beautiful, incredibly warm and open, inviting us into their humble homes, often sitting with us into the night, in small, windowless, poorly lit union offices, telling us stories of their lives as garment workers.

I am angry because of what is happening to these workers, who sew our clothes.

The workers' stories

There are 2 million garment workers in Bangladesh, and 85 per cent of them are young women, between 16 and 25 years old. Each year they sew £1.5 billion ($2.8 billion) worth of clothing for export to Europe, and another £1.08 billion ($2 billion) for the US.

Here are their stories.

Long hours and late pay

Women sewing garments for one of the best-known entertainment companies in the world are forced to work from 8 a.m. to 10 p.m., 15 hours a day, seven days a week, for just 10 pence (20 cents) an hour. They were allowed one day off in the last four months. They are cheated of their overtime pay, and paid late.

Recently, when a group of workers asked if their wages could be paid on time, the manager slapped one of them, screaming, 'How dare you come into my office?' After the manager made a call on his cell phone, five gang members carrying pistols arrived, and they punched and kicked 20 of the workers. Later the police arrived, and arrested and imprisoned eight of the workers for two weeks.

The workers face prison sentences on trumped-up charges. Of course, all the workers were fired. Their back wages were stolen. They may have to go into hiding.

No hope for the future

I spoke with a young woman who sewed baseball caps for one of the best-known sports labels in the world. The caps went to major league teams. She had worked in the factory for six years and her base wage was still just 10 cents an hour, 80 cents a day, or £2.38 ($4.42) a week. She earned 1.5 pence (3 cents) for each £10.80 ($20) cap she sewed. When I asked her how much she thought the cap sold for, she responded '20 taka' – or 18 pence (34 cents). When I told her that, no, it sold for £10.80 ($20) or more, she was shocked. She could not believe it. How was it possible that a single cap would nearly pay her whole month's wage?

'What do you hope for in your life?' I asked.

She responded, 'There are no rays of hope for me. In the future there is only darkness.'

Rotten food

In Bangladesh, when the workers are kept until 10 p.m., the factories often give the workers a 15-minute break from 6:45 p.m. to 7 p.m. and provide a free snack of a small banana and a tiny piece of cake. Many of the owners boast to their European and American buyers about this. In a sweater factory, one young man asked the owner if they could get different food, since the banana and the cake were rotten and smelled terrible. The manager responded by beating the young man, saying, 'What I give you, you will eat.' He was locked in a room and the police were called. The police arrived and photographed the 'offender'.

Impossible quotas

One girl told us that her production quota was to sew a pocket every 36 seconds, 100 each hour and 1,250 in a 12-hour shift. She sewed trousers for one of the best-known clothing labels in the world. The workers were paid about 6 pence (12 cents) for each pair of trousers they sewed.

Controlled by violence

Workers sewing clothing for one of the largest sports retailers in the world, a European company, were forced to work from 8 a.m. to 10 p.m., seven days a week. Before shipments had to go out, they were kept straight through from 8 a.m. until 3 a.m. the next day, working 19 hours in one shift. Then they slept on the factory floor, curled up next to their sewing machines. A bell would ring at 7 a.m. so that they could get ready for their next shift. They were paid 10 cents an hour. The workers reported being slapped and beaten for not reaching their production targets.

The workers went on strike, demanding one day off a week, an end to all physical abuse, and payment of at least the minimum wage. Then at 5 a.m. on the 3rd November 2003, the striking workers blocked a trailer truck trying to leave the factory. The owner called in the police, who opened fire, killing at least six people. The street ran with blood. The police attacked the workers with clubs, beating men and women. The police bound scores of young women by roping their legs together as if they were cattle. Forty-nine people were hospitalised. People outside could hear the screams and groans of the women still in the factory.

One 13-year-old child worker who was shot in the stomach said,

'I am still haunted by the terrible scenes of that night, and I can't forget the horror of the attack.'

Unsafe machinery

One young man operating a button machine had a needle go right through his finger. The manager gave him 10 taka (10 pence, or 17 cents) and told him to go home.

Illegally low pay

A girl, who could not have weighed more than 85 pounds, had been sewing women's underwear for a year. She earned about 3 pence (7 cents) an hour and 35 pence (56 cents) a day. This was less than the legal minimum wage. When I asked her how they got away with it, she responded, 'What can I do?'

Women cheated of rights

Women sewing some of the best-known labels in Europe and the US told us that they needed permission – a 'gate pass' – in order to use the bathroom, which was limited to twice a day. Women told us they were cheated of their legally required maternity leave with benefits. When they reach 35 years of age, they are forced out of the factory, as the companies want to replace them with another crop of young girls. If the workers try to organise to protest, they are beaten and fired.

One worker explained, 'We feel like prisoners. There is no value in our lives. We are like slaves. Our hands are bound and our mouths are stopped.'

Every worker told us that if the owners knew they were meeting with us, they would be fired.

Indefensible poverty

The multinationals say that while these wages may not sound like a lot to Westerners, one can live comfortably on them in Bangladesh. It is an inexpensive country, they say.

The workers took us to their homes. They live in one-room,

dirt-floored huts, perhaps 8 by 12 feet, made of scrap metal, wood and plastic. Four or more people share this one room. Everyone sleeps on a hard wooden platform raised about a foot off the ground. When it rains, these huts drip with water. In the rainy season, the workers' neighbourhoods flood, and filth and sewage wash right into their homes, often rising to within inches of their sleeping platforms.

Are the people in these huts lazy and unwilling to work for a living? Quite the opposite. A mother and her 14-year-old daughter both worked in the garment factories from 8 a.m. to 10 p.m., seven days a week. Some months they had to work as many as 15 all-night shifts lasting 19 hours until 3 a.m. But still their wages averaged only 8 pence (15 cents) an hour.

In these neighbourhoods, up to 60 people must share one out-door water pump, and the water is filthy. There is one outhouse, really just a hole in the ground, and two or three shared gas burn-ers for cooking. Early in the morning and late at night, there are long lines as people wait their turn.

In one hut, it was even worse. Two families, a total of eight peo-ple, had to share this single room. One woman living there told us she worked 15 hours a day, seven days a week. She earned about 5 pence (10 cents) an hour.

One housing complex was actually built on bamboo stilts over a stagnant, polluted lake. The entire structure was built of wood and corrugated metal, some of it rotted. The rooms were tiny, measuring 8 by 8 feet, without windows. In the summer, the rooms heat up like ovens. In the rainy season, they leak. It is noisy at all hours of the day and night. Two thousand people live there.

One garment worker held her infant. The company had not given her any maternity benefits. The baby had to eat whatever they could find. There was no special food. If the child ever got sick, they would need to borrow money to be able to go to the doctor.

The big questions

The corporations claim that they have codes of conduct which guarantee the human and worker rights of anyone anywhere in the world making their products. They ask us to trust them. They say they are seriously monitoring their contractors' plants. In reality, though, their monitoring is a joke and is failing miserably.

I want to ask the corporations: Why are your monitors not driving out at night, say at 10 p.m., or midnight, or even 2 a.m. or 3 a.m., to see your contractors' plants still operating? Why are your monitors not visiting these plants on Fridays, the Muslim holiday, to witness the plants still operating? Why do your monitors never interview workers away from the plant, in a safe location and in the presence of local human rights groups whom they trust? You know as well as I do that any worker interviewed in the factory who speaks truthfully about bad working conditions will be fired the minute you walk out of the door. Why have your monitors never asked to visit the workers in their homes? (I have done all these things, and I can tell you, it is not hard to do. You just have to have the will.) Are you ashamed of the abject poverty in which your workers are trapped? Does it not strike you as odd that there is not a single union operating with a contract in over 3,700 garment factories here, despite the abuse, excessive hours and starvation wages?

The companies must stop this current monitoring charade and get serious.

Now I want to address the World Trade Organisation (WTO), and I will not pretend to hide my anger: 2,000 new garment factories opened in Bangladesh between 1994 and 2003, while apparel exports grew by more than 300 per cent, exploding from £0.846 billion ($1.56 billion) in 1994 to £2.656 billion ($4.912 billion) in 2003. The garment industry is booming. Should this not be a good example of the magic of trade?

But then why are two million mostly young women garment

workers being left behind, stripped of their rights – in their own words, 'trapped like slaves' – paid just pennies an hour, working exhausting hours and seven-day weeks, yet living in utter misery, and thrown out, penniless and worn out, when they reach 35 years of age? What have these women done wrong? The answer is nothing. They are some of the hardest-working people in the world, and they deserve to be treated as human beings.

Trade, in and of itself, will never bring social justice. The truth is that, as unfettered corporate power grows, the workers suffer. Consider Wal-Mart, the largest company and worst sweatshop abuser in the world. Three years ago, Wal-Mart paid its contractors in Bangladesh £20.52 ($38) per dozen sports shirts they made, or £1.71 ($3.17) each. (This represents the total cost of production, including all materials, labour, overheads and profit to the contractor.) Today, for the exact same shirts, Wal-Mart pays just £19.44 ($26) per dozen, or £1.17 ($2.17) each. This cut of 54 pence ($1) per shirt amounts to a more than 30 per cent drop in the price Wal-Mart is willing to pay – and this despite the fact that over the last three years, the compounded inflation rate in Bangladesh has been 25.6 per cent.

Companies like Wal-Mart are doing this all across the developing world, virtually putting a gun to the head of local factory managers and telling them to accept the constantly lower prices or lose the desperately needed work. Behind Wal-Mart's 'everyday low prices' are workers trapped in slave labour conditions, paid starvation wages and living in utter misery.

And it could get worse. For years, the apparel trade has been governed by bilateral agreements, which have provided developing countries with a set quota, or amount of apparel, they could ship to the US or Europe. Each year, the quotas were increased. Now, the WTO's apparel and textile quotas have been lifted and millions of desperately poor garment workers risk losing their jobs. No one knows exactly what will happen over the next few decades, but here is what some leaders in the industry are imagining:

- One half of all apparel factories in the world face closure.
- The current field of 38 major apparel producer countries will be narrowed to between 12 and 15.
- The apparel industry in sub-Saharan Africa could be wiped out. The Philippines, Indonesia and Mexico will also suffer. Bangladesh will be on the borderline, although by some estimates it could lose as many as one million jobs.
- China will be the big winner, within a short time possibly accounting for 80 per cent of all apparel imports to the US. Vietnam, Pakistan and India are also expected to emerge as winners.
- Apparel prices could fall between 15 and 30 per cent.
- Millions of garment workers across the developing world, mostly young women, could find themselves thrown out in the street, jobless and penniless.
- Already weak governments could be destabilised.

This will be a race to the bottom on steroids. It will be a field day for the corporations, as standards and wages all across the developing world are lowered. More than ever before, we need fundamental human, women's and workers' rights standards and environmental protections, beneath which we will not allow the corporations to go.

Since the WTO will never be anything but a lackey to corporate interests, we, the people, need to take this into our own hands and hold the corporations accountable to respect worker rights and pay fair wages.

We need to break through to each other. There is a human being behind that label. She is our sister. That garment holds the story of her life. If we ignore it, if we do not care to understand, she suffers, and so do we. If we do not take it personally, the corporations will continue to commodify, trivialise and exploit every aspect of our lives.

After all, a consumer is first a person, a human being. We need to expose these corporations, shame them, drag them out into the light of day.

The first step

In Bangladesh, garment workers have the legal right to three months maternity leave with full pay. Yet, in over 90 per cent of the factories, where women are sewing some of the best-known labels in Europe and America, this right to maternity leave with benefits is routinely violated. For women and their infants, this is literally a matter of life and death since they have no savings to fall back on, given their below-subsistence wages.

The National Labour Committee launched a popular, grass-roots campaign to get multinationals to pledge that the factories with which they subcontract would honour the law. Eighteen major corporations signed the pledge, including Disney, Levi-Strauss, Ikea, Gap, Littlewoods, Sears and Reebok – with the notable exception of Wal-Mart.

Our aim must be to urge Western governments to respect the poor countries' right to choose their own trade policies, to demand that they stop pushing countries to open their economies through WTC policies that are biased towards rich countries and their corporations, because while their policies remain, poverty cannot become history.

This dehumanisation of the new global workforce is emerging as the overwhelming moral crisis of the twenty-first century. This issue has become the great new civil rights justice movement of our time.

Never think the answer to this dilemma is in the words, 'Well, at least they have a job.' It is not a job when you do not get a day off a week, or you work 15 hours a day. It is not a job when sick days are not allowed, or when you have no rights, and if you speak out to protest or ask for legal rights, you are fired. It is as damn near to slavery as is possible.

As people, as consumers, we will have the chance to hold corporations accountable, one right at a time.

This might seem like a small step. But as the race to the bottom accelerates in the global sweatshop economy, we, the people, have to find some way to take back our world and put a human face on it. This is at least a start, and one that, together, we can win.

Dame Anita Roddick

Dame Anita Roddick started The Body Shop in 1976 in Brighton, England. Thirty years on, The Body Shop – one of the most widely recognised and respected brands in the world – has 2,020 stores in 52 different countries. What distinguishes The Body Shop and Anita from other global businesses and entrepreneurs is a core dedication to community trade and human rights causes. Roddick is a key pioneer of socially responsible business, proving that commerce with a conscience is not only a moral imperative, but also a competitive advantage. She was named a Dame of the Order of the British Empire in 2003.

An outspoken opponent of economic globalisation, Roddick is the only executive of a major global corporation who was tear-gassed in the streets of Seattle in 1999. She has written several books, including the autobiographical *Body and Soul* and *Business as Unusual*, and was editor of the popular 2001 title *Take it Personally: How to Make Conscious Choices to Change the World*.

Her websites are www.anitaroddick.com and www.takeitpersonally.com.

8: Bonded labour in Pakistan

Michele Lombardo, Just Law International

What is bonded labour?

Pakistan's constitution declares:

> Slavery is non-existent and forbidden and no law shall permit or facil-
> itate its introduction into Pakistan in any form. All forms of forced
> labour and traffic in human beings are prohibited. No child below the
> age of 14 years shall be engaged in any factory or mine or any other
> hazardous employment.[1]

Nevertheless, in twenty-first-century Pakistan, between 5 and 20
million men, women and children are enslaved in an archaic,
inhumane and illegal system of bonded labour. The system is
most prevalent in agriculture and the back-breaking work of
Pakistan's brick kilns, but is also active in mines, the carpet industry and domestic service.

Bonded labour is proliferated through an endemic and widespread system of *peshgi* (advance money), which exploits impoverished and minority groups.

The poorest of Pakistan's poor approach a wealthy *zamindar*
(landlord) either directly or through a *jamadar* (broker) for a small

---

[1] Constitution of Pakistan, Article 11 (1–3). www.nrb.gov.pk/constitutional_
and_legal/constitution/.

loan. The loan is granted as a cash advance that the debtor agrees to pay back through labour. To the debtor, the nominal amount means the difference between life and death for a sick child or starving family member.

By accepting the *peshgi*, the debtor, with his wife and children, are bound to the creditor/employer until the entire debt is paid. The unconscionable bonded labour system is designed to ensure that debts are never paid off, as arbitrary (and illegal) interest accumulates at extravagant rates without the understanding or consent of poor, illiterate debtors.

Debtors, along with their families, are kept in perpetual bondage to these modern-day slave owners. The employer pays a single, despicably low wage to the husband, while the wife and children are not compensated for their work. Typically, 50 per cent of the wage is withheld under the pretence that it is applied to the family's debt.

The brick kilns

In Pakistan's brick kilns, families begin their hard labour before dawn and work late into the evening – slaving for more than 12 hours each day, seven days a week, for less than 1,800 rupees (approximately £17) per month. The UN's International Labour Office's (ILO) 2005 global report on forced labour found that 40 per cent of brick kiln workers in Punjab and sharecroppers in Sindh

> had no understanding of their creditors' calculations concerning debt, the terms of which were dictated unilaterally by the employer or landlord. Many confirmed that they were not free to seek alternative employment while their debts remained unpaid. Between one-fifth and one-third also reported verbal or physical coercion on the part of the landlord or employer. Household illiteracy was a key indicator of both destitution and bondage.[2]

---

[2] ILO, Report of the Director General, 'A global alliance against forced labour: Global Report under the Follow-Up to the ILO Declaration on Fundamental Principles and Rights at Work', May 2005, p. 31, www.ilo.org/dyn/declaris/ DECLARATIONWEB.DOWNLOAD_BLOB?Var_DocumentID=5059.

Bonded labourers are usually members of the Christian minority or descended from low-caste Hindu families in India. They are easy to control, less aware of their rights or willing to fight for them, and the powerful rural landowners and kiln bosses can count on local government and police to protect their interests.

The *bhatta* (brick kilns) are located on the outskirts of major cities and towns and operate almost exclusively on the basis of debt bondage. The lands are covered in the thick soot being constantly expelled from enormous black chimneys. Fathers, mothers and children of all ages work under gruelling, dangerous conditions in the blistering heat of summer and the punishing cold of winter.

The day begins with *patheras* (primarily women and children) preparing *katcha* (raw) bricks, and most families are expected to make approximately 1,000 each day.

The unbaked bricks are then loaded onto donkeys by a second group called *bharaiwalas*, and taken to the kiln. The most difficult work is then performed by *jalaiwalas* – adult men who feed coal into the hellish furnace and stand beside it while the bricks are baked. For more than 12 hours each day, even in the most intense heat of summer, these men continually feed and stoke the fires, and load one brick after another.[3]

The final group of workers, called *nakasiwalas*, remove the finished bricks and transport them to the market. The workers are supervised by *jamadars*, and the worksite itself is usually under surveillance by guards – often armed – called *chowkidars*.[4]

---

[3] See Human Rights Watch, 'Contemporary Forms of Slavery in Pakistan', July 1995, www.hrw.org/reports/1995/Pakistan.htm. See also, Construction, Forestry, Mining and Energy Union (CFMEU) of Australia, 'Barbarism and Slavery in 2006: Gross Human Rights Atrocities Against Pakistan Brick-Kiln Workers', 11 April, 2006, www.cfmeu-construction-nsw.com.au/pdf/tapakistan.pdf.

[4] Human Rights Watch, 'Contemporary Forms of Slavery'.

Filth and poverty

In November 2005, I visited a brick kiln outside Lahore as part of a Jubilee Campaign USA delegation invited by Joseph Francis, of the Centre for Legal Aid, Assistance and Settlement (CLAAS). It was early afternoon when we arrived, so the mammoth furnaces were already spouting billowing, black smoke into the dense and eerily tinted air.

First to greet us were barefoot children covered from head to toe in thick dust and soot, their clothing torn, tattered and stained. One little girl carried an even smaller boy on her hip throughout our visit. Another young boy had an eye infection.

The men of the area were sun-worn and covered in thick dust and soot like their children. One rugged worker stood on a literal field of fire, where every six inches or so there was a round metal lid covering the flames below. When he lifted a lid with a metal rod, the burning flames leapt above the surface. To close the lid, the man would stamp on it with his handmade sandals – planks of wood with fabric nailed across to hold them in place. Children ran onto the burning field, and the man quickly chased them off. There was other work for them to do – loading wheelbarrows, donkeys and trucks, scraping the earth, or helping women with laundry.

Nearly all the women we saw at that time of the day were washing clothes in muddy streams. They were also covered in soot, their skin tanned and hard from the unforgiving sun and the chemicals emanating from the chimney at the centre of their lives.

One of the men showed us their living quarters. Each family's home was a small, square brick hut with a single brick-sized hole in one wall. Inside were two wooden cots with a single blanket on each.

We observed a young boy herding sheep, old men adjusting the current of a man-made spring, a woman crouched down scraping ground to loosen it while her naked baby rolled in the dirt, children and youths stamping bricks and lining them in rows, and children carrying bricks one at a time to wheelbarrows and trucks.

Although the *jamadar* allowed us to speak with the bonded labourers, he watched our every move. We learned that those enslaved at this location included both Christians and impoverished Muslims. None of the men we spoke to had details of their debt or the amount they had paid off, and they were far from knowledgeable with regards to the terms under which they were bonded. Some women confided that they had been 'punished' and 'touched'.

The law – an ongoing struggle

In February 2006, the Human Rights Commission of Pakistan (HRCP) reported:

> A rapid assessment on bonded labour, carried out by the ministry of labour, ILO and other organizations late last year, found almost one million bonded labourers in 4,000 brick kilns across the country. Many kilns were unregistered, with virtually no safeguards for workers. Physical and sexual abuse, especially of children, was common with women also reporting rape by kiln owners.[5]

Children of the brick kilns are denied even basic education and are unaware that they are legally free to leave their lives of bondage and to avail themselves of training that could help them secure outside employment.

Nevertheless, on the basis of Article 11, Pakistan's Supreme Court ruled against brick kiln owners in the case of Darshan Masih v. State, PLD 1990, Supreme Court 513. The court legally abolished the *peshgi* system, although it fell short of emancipating the victims. The decision allowed 'employers' to continue loaning workers up to one week's salary, and it failed to forgive bonded labourers their past and existing debts – outlawing only the future practice of *peshgi*.

---

[5] Human Rights Commission of Pakistan (HRCP), 'State of Human Rights in 2005', February 2006, Section 5-3, Labour, p. 231, www.hrcp-web.org/ar_home_o5.cfm.

Loopholes and apathy

This gaping loophole was presumably plugged by the Bonded Labour System (Abolition) Act of 1992 (BLAA). The Act outlawed the system, freed labourers and cancelled outstanding debts.

Unfortunately, it has never been diligently enforced by Pakistan's government against powerful brick kiln bosses and landowners. Writs of habeas corpus are filed on an ongoing basis in Pakistan's High Courts, asking that bonded labourers and their families be set free from the clutches of cruel masters who are blatantly and with impunity keeping slaves, despite legislation outlawing both bonded labour and child labour. Fourteen years after the Act, the US Department of State reported:

> Bonded labourers were often unable to determine when their debts were fully paid. Those who escaped often faced retaliation from former employers. Some bonded labourers returned to their former status after being freed due to a lack of alternative livelihoods. Although the police arrested violators of the law against bonded labour, many such individuals bribed the police to release them. Human rights groups reported that landlords in rural Sindh maintained as many as 50 private jails housing some 4,500 bonded labourers. Ties between such landlords and influential politicians hampered effective elimination of bonded labour.[6]

'The continued existence of bonded labour shows that the authorities simply have no wish to see it end or to enforce the law,' Asma Jahangir, a leading lawyer, UN rapporteur and chairperson of the HRCP, told the UN Office for the Co-ordination of Humanitarian Affairs.[7] An appeal seeking the upholding of the law on bonded labour is now before the Supreme Court. It was moved by HRCP after the Sindh High Court in 2002 dismissed the petitions of 94 bonded farm workers.[8]

---

[6] US Department of State, 'Pakistan Country Report on Human Rights Practices – 2005', 8 March 2006, www.state.gov/g/drl/rls/hrrpt/2005/61710.htm.

[7] See UN Office for the Co-ordination of Humanitarian Affairs, IRINnews.org, 'Pakistan: Focus on kidney sales by bonded labourers', 7 April 2005, www.irinnews.org/print.asp?ReportID=46508. [8] Ibid.

In 2005, the UN observed that bonded labourers were taking extreme measures to pay off *peshgi* debts they do not legally owe and had sold kidneys to buy their freedom.[9]

> Each kidney, bought from donors on average for between $1,000 and $2,000, depending on the age and health of the donor, is sold to rich recipients for up to 10 times that amount.
>
> An increased number of visitors from abroad are travelling to the country to fly out with a brand new kidney, and Pakistan is now thought to be a growing centre of global 'organ tourism'.[10]

Success and danger hand in hand

CLAAS has filed multiple petitions to free illegally enslaved brick kiln workers, and secured the release of 351 such individuals in June 2005. The workers, including women and children as young as seven, toiled in 16 brick kilns in Sheikhupura, Mandi Bahauddin and Lahore, and testified in Lahore's High Court.

Three days after these people's release, on the 17th June 2005, a clearly premeditated drive-by shooting targeted CLAAS's director Joseph Francis and another staff member, although both escaped unharmed. The attack illustrates the grave danger faced by those who undertake such advocacy.

A rising movement

The HRCP, Anti-Slavery International and other NGOs and labour unions have also been tireless advocates on the issue, and there is an amazing rising movement among bonded labourers themselves.

In early 2006, thousands of bonded brick kiln workers organised strikes and protests demanding better wages, kiln registration, 'an end to the humiliation of women workers and the withdrawal of all false cases registered by the police at the behest of the owners'.[11]

---

[9] Ibid.

[10] Ibid.

[11] See Europe Solidaire Sans Frontieres, 'Brick Labourers: Victory in Sight', 4 May

Kiln owners retaliated by bringing criminal cases against the protesters and many were beaten and arrested by police acting in collusion with the owners.[12] The strike ended eight days later, with government assurances that the BLAA would be implemented.[13] Only time will tell if these are more than hollow promises.

Powerful pressure needed

Slavery in Pakistan – whether through forced labour, trafficking in human beings, or hazardous child labour – cannot be tolerated at any level of government or society. These practices rob victims of their dignity and violate the most fundamental of human rights. But advocacy within Pakistan alone is not enough. The country receives enormous financial support from the US and Europe, while its government portrays Pakistan as a nation committed to protecting human rights.

No nation that turns a blind eye to the enslavement of its most vulnerable people can be considered a protector of human rights. And to reward such a country financially without requiring it to uphold its obligations to human rights is both foolish and alarming. Monetary and political pressure must be exerted on Pakistan's government. And it is up to free people everywhere to insist that their representatives exert such pressure. It is essential that slavery in every form be abolished, and that we who are not enslaved support those on the frontline of the struggle.

2006, www.europe-solidaire.org/article.php3?id_article=2143. See also, International Viewpoint, 'Pakistan Brick kiln worker revolt against slave labour', March 2006, www.internationalviewpoint.org/article.php3?id_article=999.

[12] International Viewpoint, 'Pakistan Brick kiln worker revolt'.

[13] See Europe Solidaire Sans Frontieres, 'The Bhatta Workers strike ends with a victory note', 27 April 2006, www.europe-solidaire.org/article_impr. php3?id_article=2022.

MICHELE LOMBARDO

Michele Lombardo is an attorney in the US, specialising in asylum and refugee law. She does advocacy work with Jubilee Campaign USA, writing extensively on issues pertaining to international human rights, religious freedom and persecution abroad. Michele is the co-author, along with Lord Alton of Liverpool, of the book *Passion and Pain: the Suffering Church*, which was also made into a 13-part television series. Visit www.justlawintl.com.

9: Burma: Forced labour and forced conscription

Benedict Rogers, Christian Solidarity Worldwide

Forced labour

As he told his story, the 15-year-old Shan boy looked into my eyes. 'Please tell the world to put pressure on the military regime to stop killing its people. Please tell the world not to forget us.'

I had walked for over eight hours through the jungle from Thailand, before I reached the Shan village where I met him. He was one of over a million internally displaced people (IDP) in eastern Burma who have been forced to flee their villages to escape the Burma Army. Since 1996, over 2,800 villages in eastern Burma alone have been destroyed or forcibly relocated.

He told me how he had seen his father shot dead in front of him, as he worked in his paddy field. He waited until the soldiers had left, and then brought his father's body back for burial. A few weeks later the military, known as the Tatmadaw, struck again. This time they burned down the entire village, killed most of the villagers, and took this boy as a forced porter. He was made to walk long distances for three days, carrying heavy loads of army equipment and rice. He was denied food and water. At the end of three days, he collapsed from exhaustion, dehydration and hunger. When he refused, or was unable, to continue walking, the soldiers beat him unconscious and moved on. When he regained consciousness, he made his escape.

Forced conscription

A few days after meeting this boy, I met another child, Kyow Zeya, a Burman, with another story to tell. At the age of eleven, he had been standing at a bus stop in Rangoon, the capital of Burma, on his way to visit his aunt, when a truckload of Tatmadaw soldiers pulled up alongside him, grabbed him and told him he had to join the army. I asked him if he was given a choice, to which he replied, 'My choice was to join the army, or to go to jail.' He has not seen his family since.

After his capture, Kyow Zeya was taken to a military camp, where he saw at least 30 children of a similar age. After eight months, he was transferred to a training camp and forced to undergo five months of military training. He was then sent to Papun District, Karen State, and to the front line in the Burma Army's offensive against the Karen ethnic group. In a unit of 30 soldiers, he told me, 15 were his age.

Kyow Zeya spent eight months on the front line and witnessed many attacks on villages. He saw Karen villagers being rounded up and forced to work as porters for the army. Burma Army soldiers were under orders to burn, loot, rape and kill. He was beaten regularly, often for simple mistakes such as failing to carry his gun. He was warned that if he ever tried to escape and fell into the hands of the Karen resistance, they would torture and kill him. Even though he believed this propaganda and feared the Karen, after eight months in the Burma Army he had had enough. 'I did not want to live any more,' he told me.

He made an escape, and was almost immediately captured by the Karen. But in contrast to the way the Burma Army depicted the Karen, Kyow Zeya said they have looked after him and given him sanctuary. 'I feel safe and free and loved. But life in the Burma Army was like hell,' he said.

'It is not good for a child to be a soldier,' he added. 'Tell the international community to speak to the regime, to tell them not to grab children and force them to be soldiers.'

A brutal regime

According to Human Rights Watch, Burma has the highest number of forcibly conscripted child soldiers in the world – over 70,000, making up at least 20 per cent of the Burma Army.

Forced labour and forced conscription of child soldiers are modern forms of slavery – and they are characteristic of the brutal, illegal regime which rules Burma. The State Peace and Development Council (SPDC) is a military junta which follows a succession of military regimes since General Ne Win took power in a coup in 1962. In elections in 1990, the National League for Democracy (NLD) led by Nobel Laureate Aung San Suu Kyi won over 80 per cent of the parliamentary seats, but the regime's response was to ignore the results, imprison the victors and intensify its grip on power. Aung San Suu Kyi remains under house arrest, and over 1,100 prisoners of conscience are in jail, subjected to grotesque forms of torture. Some, such as Aye Myint and Su Su Nway, have been jailed for filing complaints of forced labour to the International Labour Organisation (ILO).

Throughout Burma, civilians of all ethnicities – from the Burman majority population and the Karen, Karenni, Shan, Mon, Chin, Kachin, Rakhine, Rohingya and other ethnic nationality groups – have been used for forced labour. One Kachin refugee in India told me that forced labour occurs 'on a daily basis'. The evidence is widespread and the practice is systematic. According to the International Confederation of Trade Unions (ICFTU), 'In Burma, on any given day, several hundred thousand men, women, children and elderly people are forced to work against their will by the country's military rulers . . . Refusal to work may lead to being detained, tortured, raped, or killed.' The ILO has reported the continued use of forced labour, and has passed resolutions condemning the practice in Burma.

Throughout history, tyrannical regimes have used forced labour to subjugate, terrorise and control their citizens.

The best-known example of this is Adolf Hitler and Nazi Germany. The Nazis established a horrific system of concentration camps, which were separate from the extermination camps in which Jews were gassed. In the concentration camps, prisoners were forced to work, and at the same time were subjected to terrible conditions – little food, poor sanitation, beatings and torture. The Germans also established slave labour camps in the countries they occupied. '*Arbeit Macht Frei*' ('Work Makes You Free') was a chilling slogan used by the Nazis.

The Japanese also used prison labour during the Second World War, particularly from prisoners of war. The most famous example, dramatised in film, is the use of captured British soldiers to build the bridge over the River Kwai in Burma.

The Soviet Union is another prime example of the use of slavery. Dissidents were sent to the 'gulags' or labour camps, mainly in Siberia, described most powerfully in Alexander Solzhenitsyn's *The Gulag Archipelago*.

In China, the extensive use of prison labour has been well documented by former prisoner Harry Wu, who spent 19 years in the prison camps. Known as the *laogai* ('re-education through labour'), China's network of labour camps is used to produce goods for the international market. Harry Wu's Laogai Research Foundation continues to document and report the use of prison labour.

North Korea has copied the Soviet gulag model, and information has trickled out about the horrific conditions in the North Korean gulag. Satellite photographs and testimonies from defectors provide a picture of an extensive network of slave labour, documented most powerfully in David Hawk's report, 'The Hidden Gulag: Exposing North Korea's Prison Camps'.

The military can order ordinary people to be taken from their homes at a moment's notice, or issue written orders demanding that a village contribute labour. Villagers are shackled and used to build roads, bridges and buildings, or to porter for the military. In Chin State, prisoners in labour camps are used to plough fields, yoked around the neck like oxen and fed banana leaves. In Karen State, in a major offensive in 2006 that caused the displacement of over 18,000 civilians, at least 800 people were captured in one area alone and used for forced labour, according to the Free Burma Rangers.

Religious persecution

The overwhelming majority of Chins are Christians, and the regime uses this against them. The military sometimes disrupts Sunday church services and takes the pastor for forced labour. They have forced Chin Christians to tear down crosses built on mountain-tops and to construct Buddhist pagodas in their place – contributing, against their will, not only labour but money to the costs of the pagodas' construction.

Like the Chin, the Kachin are also about 90 per cent Christian, and their faith is the subject of attack. Often the SPDC deliberately demands forced labour during Christian festivals. In Sabungte, for example, Tatmadaw soldiers ordered villagers to porter for the army from the 20th December 2003 until the 9th January 2004, during the Christmas and New Year period. They had to carry 55-pound packs of rice, ammunition and mortars. In Hmun Halh, in July 2003, troops entered a church in the middle of a Sunday service and ordered the church leaders to leave immediately to serve as porters.

Forced relocation

Sometimes the military uses prisoners for labour. But the regime also uses the forced relocation of villages, ensuring a ready pool of forced labour under the constant control of the military. Hundreds of thousands of villagers in eastern Burma, particularly in Karenni State, have been forced to abandon their homes and move, at gunpoint, to new relocation camps. On the 25 December 2003, in Maw Chi, Karenni State, the divisional commander told villagers to move to a relocation site at Mahntahlaying within ten days and warned that anyone who failed to obey would be shot. However, three days later the SPDC soldiers returned and ordered people to move immediately. Villagers who went to Mahntahlaying were forced to repair the road and provide their own food; no health care or education was provided. Some villagers escaped, and over 3,000 IDPs are hiding in the jungle, constantly on the move. 'They have to run, in order to stay alive,' said one Karenni spokesman. 'They are fed up with moving all the time. They have no homes, no health care, no food and no education – if this is not ethnic cleansing, what is?'

In relocation camps, forced labour on construction projects is closely controlled by SPDC soldiers. On average, one soldier watches over 10–15 forced labourers, beating them if they stop working. Villagers have to provide their own tools, building materials and food, and are forced to work from 6 a.m. until dusk, making it difficult to find food supplies.

Porters are forced to carry heavy loads for long distances, allowed little food, water or rest. In one case, a man was reportedly ordered to carry 100 kilos of rice. In order to comply, he had to involve his children. In Karen and Karenni States, it is common practice for SPDC soldiers to form a column. They divide the porters into groups of three, interspersing them among the soldiers, protecting the soldiers from ambush.

Sexual slavery

Human trafficking and sexual slavery are other forms of slavery in Burma today. Kachin women have been sold as 'wives' in China, according to 'Driven Away', a 2005 report. Mon women have been taken by the Burma Army and kept as sex slaves in military camps, where they are repeatedly gang-raped, beaten and forced to take part in 'fashion and beauty shows' for the troops, according to the report 'Catwalk to the Barracks'.

Human minesweepers

Civilians are used as human minesweepers, forced to walk across fields of landmines to clear the mines for the military, but losing their limbs – and sometimes their lives – in the process. Is that not a form of modern-day slavery too?

I have met some of the survivors, seen their stumps, touched their wounds. The use of human minesweepers must rank as one of the most barbaric forms of slavery ever.

'We cannot turn aside'

Burma is a nation imprisoned and enslaved. If he were alive today, William Wilberforce would, I believe, count the forced conscription of children into the military, the use of forced labour and human minesweepers, and sexual enslavement, as forms of slavery. When he spoke in the House of Commons on the slave trade, he said these words: 'We can no longer plead ignorance. We cannot turn aside.' We must hear Wilberforce's words for Burma today.

Yet despite the modern-day slavery in Burma, there are inspiring flickers of light and hope in the darkness. A Karen pastor, Reverend Dr Simon, for example, had to give up a good position as a seminary professor and theologian to flee to the refugee camps in Thailand. But once there, he put his time to good use. Seeing the needs of young people for education, he started a Bible school. He now offers bachelor's degrees in divinity, approved by the Baptist World Alliance. And he composes meditations, in English, that speak of his people's suffering and hope:

> They call us a displaced people,
> But praise God; we are not misplaced.

> They say they see no hope for our future,
> But praise God; our future is as bright as the promises of God.

They say they see the life of our people is a misery,
But praise God; our life is a mystery.

For what they say is what they see,
And what they see is temporal.
But ours is the eternal.
All because we put ourselves
In the hands of the God we trust.

BENEDICT ROGERS

Benedict Rogers is a journalist and human rights advocate, and author of *A Land Without Evil: Stopping the Genocide of Burma's Karen People* (Monarch, 2004). He works with the international human rights organisation Christian Solidarity Worldwide, and has travelled extensively in Burma, East Timor, China, India, Pakistan, Sri Lanka, Armenia and Nagorno Karabakh. He contributes regularly to publications such as the *Wall Street Journal* and *Crisis,* and from 1997 to 2002 worked as a journalist in Hong Kong. He is deputy chairman of the Conservative Party Human Rights Commission. He has appeared regularly on radio and television, spoken at the White House, the US Congress, the Heritage Foundation, the Foreign Correspondents Club of Hong Kong and in churches and conferences around the world, and regularly briefs governments and parliamentarians on international human rights issues.

Christian Solidarity Worldwide (CSW) is a human rights organisation specialising in religious freedom. CSW works on behalf of those persecuted for their Christian beliefs and promotes religious liberty for all.

For more information, see www.csw.org.uk and www.ben-rogers.org.uk.

10: Lobbying at the United Nations Human Rights Commission for trafficked North Korean refugees

Ann Buwalda, Founder, Just Law International

Trafficking of vulnerable refugees is a horrific form of modern slavery and nowhere is this more acute than the plight of North Koreans who seek sanctuary in China. Instead of refuge and protection, North Korean women and girls find only terror and abuse and men face bonded labour conditions or worse.

The plight of North Korean refugees

Over 200,000 refugees from the Democratic Peoples Republic of Korea (DPRK) now live in China, half of them women. Interviews with refugees who have reached South Korea reveal that at least 90 per cent or more of those women are trafficked and forced into sexual servitude as prostitutes, brides to Chinese men, or sexual entertainers in clubs.

Young, a 29-year-old woman, fled to China with her daughter to escape starvation and brutal beatings from her violent husband in the DPRK. The *Washington Post* reported how Young avoided border guards, bravely crossed the Tumen River, and safely arrived in China at a house she believed would provide her with shelter. Instead, to her horror, the owners of the home offered her for sale to a Chinese farmer. Young managed to escape, but she was eventually sold into a life of sexual abuse. Forced to work in a bar, she suffered from sexual assault, physical abuse, utter humiliation and ridicule by the men. Once more she escaped, but was recaptured by Chinese gang members who forced her into a degrading life of prostitution.

Throughout this abuse, Young had no opportunity to obtain legal protection. Chinese authorities not only tolerate the trafficking, but they are complicit in it.

Human rights violations

Most countries, including China, generally are sensitive to expressions of human rights concerns raised by the international community. The reaction of countries to international pressure varies along the spectrum – from denial and retribution to an openness to dialogue and change. On certain issues, including the presence of North Korean defectors in their country, China has expressed denial of wrongdoing and committed retribution against those who undertake advocacy. The DPRK has completely ignored international statements of any kind, continuing its human rights violations unabated. Yet, by shining light on the human rights violations within the DPRK and repeatedly raising the failure of China both to abide by its international obligation of non-refoulement (forced return contrary to treaty obligations) and to provide unimpeded access to all refugees, bilateral and multilateral relations have been affected and various United Nations mechanisms reflect the violations as a constant reminder that the world community does not approve. Our advocacy efforts have had a significant impact.

Advocacy interventions

At the United Nations Human Rights Commission sessions in 2003, 2004 and 2005, Jubilee Campaign used its consultative status, and worked with Korean-based and other human rights organisations, to raise the plight of these modern-day sex slaves. Through our advocacy efforts, in each of those years, we secured a resolution which condemned human rights violations in North Korea, including demands that China put a stop to the trafficking of North Korean women. As with most advocacy interventions, the process consisted of progressive steps. Introduced by the European Union for the first time ever in 2003, the Commission passed the Resolution by a fair margin after accredited Jubilee Campaign delegates personally spoke to the representatives of every country.

The following year, the EU recommended the appointment of a special rapporteur to investigate violations of human rights and improve monitoring co-operation of the World Food Programme's efforts in North Korea. Our advocacy efforts included facilitating the testimony of a North Korean defector. Won Cheol Kang described his escape to freedom in South Korea, including his capture and refoulement by China back to the DPRK, where he spent three months in the Nongpo Detention Centre in Chungjin City. Eleven prisoners died during his internment there.

In her address to the UN Human Rights Commission in 2004, Jubilee Campaign's Sue Yoon-Logan declared, 'Chinese authorities have prosecuted humanitarian aid workers under its human trafficking laws, simply for providing safe-haven to North Korean refugees in China. However, Chinese authorities fail to prosecute the real perpetrators who traffic women and force them into depraved and inhumane situations.'

Later in the session, Professor Jae Won, Jubilee Campaign's representative from Handong International Law School in South Korea, also addressed the UN Commission and provided factual evidence that China is systematically eradicating any infrastructure of humanitarian relief on its side of the border. China offers substantial bounty money on the head of displaced North Koreans and considerably more for capturing aid workers. Consequently, China has arrested scores of monitors and humanitarian workers. 'The Chinese solution to its refugee problem is to eliminate its refugee population in a campaign to cleanse all North Koreans and remove the embarrassment,' Professor Won told the UN Commission.

The prevailing cause of North Koreans leaving their country is the failed food policy. Foremost is the need for structural reform within the DPRK's food distribution priorities. The DPRK distributes food to soldiers first, thereby discriminating against the general population. In 2005, I told the UN Commission, 'Food from the international community should not be used as a weapon, nor should it be used as a weapon by the DPRK itself on its own population. Food should be distributed, especially to children under five and women, according to need rather than political status.'

During the 2005 Commission session, Jubilee Campaign co-sponsored a special parallel meeting that screened the first-ever video footage of public executions of refouled defectors. This video, first broadcast the previous month on Japanese television, provided evidence of an outdoor public trial, pronouncement of a guilty verdict, the prisoner's sentence to death by a 'judge', and the victim's execution by firing squad. Children can be seen in the public audience, as can police who prodded the crowd into viewing position.

Elaborating on the report that he delivered to the Commission earlier that same week, the United Nation's special rapporteur on the situation of human rights in the DPRK, Professor Vitit Muntarbhorn, stated, 'It is important to make it known as I have done that those who came out of the DPRK are refugees and entitled to international protection. They are entitled to the basic right of non-refoulement. We should not be deluded by terms such as "illegal immigrants". They are persecuted, they are protected by international law, and they must receive protection.' He went on to say, 'The UNHCR is to give this protection. The UNHCR does not have access in many situations, including with the North Korean refugees.' Nearly two years after these comments were made, China has tacitly permitted the UNHCR to have access to a small number of North Korean defectors on its territory. Without international advocacy pressuring China as well as the UNHCR and its supporting governments, even that incremental change would not have happened. International advocacy has had a sustained effect even on the Six Party talks involving nuclear disarmament, with calls for a 'Helsinki approach' to human rights in North Korea taken seriously.

Although in March 2006 the United Nations dissolved the Human Rights Commission, it was a useful body in which to raise specific human rights violations. Its successor UN body, the Human Rights Council, is hoped to possess an even more credible approach to human rights protection. As long as the despotic North Korean government remains in power, the plight of its citizens fleeing oppression will remain a priority to address within the Council.

ANN BUWALDA

Ann Buwalda is a leading, highly respected human rights attorney in Washington, DC and founded Just Law International PC, a law firm emphasising legal advice in immigration law. She established Jubilee Campaign's office in the United States in 1996 and serves as its director. Ann graduated from Regent University School of Law in 1990 and earned masters degrees in public policy and communications from Regent University in 1991. Since 2002, she has served as an adjunct professor of human rights and refugee law at Handong International Law School in Pohang, Korea, and she is a member of the Virginia and Pennsylvania bars.

For more information, see www.justlawintl.com and www.jubileecampaign.org.

PART TWO: BRITAIN'S SLAVE TRADE

Maafa – a Kiswahili term meaning an event of great disaster, a calamity or terrible occurrence.

Almost every event of my life made an impression on my mind, and influenced my conduct. I early accustomed myself to look at the hand of God in the minutest occurrence, and to learn from it a lesson of morality and religion . . . after all, what makes any event important, unless by its observation we become better and wiser, and learn 'to do justly, to love mercy, and walk humbly before God'?

Olaudah Equiano, *Interesting Narrative*

11: The transatlantic slave trade and how it ended

Danny Smith, Founder, Jubilee Campaign, Jubilee Action

Slavery through the ages

There have always been slaves.

Slavery has existed throughout human history and can be traced back to the origins of civilisation and biblical times.

The ancient world accepted the practice of slavery, and slaves were essential to the economy and society of almost every early civilisation. It was taken for granted, an unquestioned fact of everyday life.

There were slaves in the world's first city of Mesopotamia – modern-day Iraq – and in early civilisations in Africa, Arabia, China and India. Egyptians sent expeditions down the River Nile to seize slaves, and temple art celebrates the capture of slaves in battle.

The Bible records incidents of slavery: Joseph, famous for his technicolour coat, was a teenager when he was sold into slavery by his jealous brothers. Egypt's Pharaoh enslaved the Israelites to attain his scheme of greater cities and to build the pyramids.

Solomon used forced labour for various ventures. Job wrote of domestic slavery; he subtly condemned the inequalities that separated master and slave, and could have been an abolitionist.

Slavery was common amongst the nomadic Arabs, seafaring Vikings, Native Americans and pre-Columbus, among the Aztec, Inca and Maya cultures. In early societies, all slaves worked for the temple or the palace, the two dominant institutions in the city.

There was a trade in slaves from Africa to Arabia long before Islam took hold and under Sultans and Islamic traders, untold numbers were taken to the Middle East over the centuries. Over one million Europeans, mainly women, were taken captive. About 1,000 slaves were imported into Europe each year. Slave markets were thriving, bustling enterprises. There were slaves of all colours from all countries around the known world.

The characteristics of slaves

Slaves were easy to recognise: they were under the control of another person, group, entity or state. The main purpose for enslaving people was to secure forced labour. Slaves were prisoners of war, captives, concubines, given in marriage, offered as debts, used in agriculture and in warfare. The slaves' physical bodies were considered the property of their owner, under his control, dominated by his command. Since ancient times, slaves were treated as property, chattel, goods, objects, products, merchandise, stock, commodities, things; as a result, they could be bought, sold, traded, leased, given as gifts or to settle debts, branded and tattooed. The slaves belonged to their owners just like any other possessions, and because they were regarded as possessions, slaves had no rights. Usually there were ethnic differences between slaves and slave owners, who considered themselves superior. Enslaving their own ethnic groups was unusual, with seventeenth- and eighteenth-century Russia one of the exceptions.

The prospect of slavery

Slavery became possible within early cultures once three concepts had developed. First, the idea of personal property had to be established. The fundamental essence of slavery is that one person is owned or controlled by another. Second, people understood from the experience of domesticated animals that they were a source of food and power. If a single animal could increase a person's own industry, one could imagine the impact made by a human workforce in a similar but more focused function. Third, communities had to absorb a concept of war, since prisoners of war were always the prime source of slaves.

The invention of democracy in a culture of slavery

Slavery increased in Greece with the rise of city-states, colonisation, the introduction of coined money as a way of exchange, and the commercial production of cotton. In the fifth century BC, as the demand for agricultural slaves increased, Athens had more slaves than free citizens. The Greeks divided slaves into three categories: public, temple and private.

The role of slaves varied considerably. Some were serfs, the descendants of an aboriginal population bound to the land and their masters. In industrialised city-states, some held official positions, in the mint and the police force; one had custody of the state archives. They inevitably took on the same work as their master, as furniture makers, vase painters, and so on.

Greek law gave slave owners almost total power over their slaves, who were regarded as the property of their masters rather than citizens of Greece. They had no rights in courts of law.

Slaves could buy their freedom, but could never become Greek citizens – the exception being Pasion, who served a banking firm faithfully. After his owner's death, he won his freedom, citizenship and the right to run the bank.

It is a paradox that Greek philosophers such as Socrates, Homer and Plato created the fundamental principles of freedom and liberty while being totally dependent on the use of slaves, and that slavery was embedded in society just as democracy was rising.

Plato's analysis of society was divided into several classes, but slaves were not included. Aristotle defined a slave as 'any person who belongs to another' and justified slavery by speculating that nature had made a free man different from a slave. He wrote, 'Some should rule and others be ruled. Humanity is divided into two: the masters and the slaves.'

Aristotle's doctrine of conflict, in *Politics*, declared that it was ethical to enslave prisoners taken in a just war. In *Ethics*, he suggested that social justice could exist only between equals, avoiding the issue of slaves. Aristotle made a huge impact in medieval Europe, but his theories carried the seeds of racism which arose in later centuries.

The Roman Empire's slave society

By 146 BC, the Romans were the undisputed masters of the civilised world. Under Rome, Europe was united in a political entity with one currency, one legal system, one military authority and one supreme state.

The Roman army needed food, cities needed to be rebuilt, landowners needed help with cultivation, and the demand for instant, cheap labour could be met in one simple way: with slaves.

In the early years, most Romans worked their own small farms, but the Punic Wars changed their society dramatically. As Romans started enslaving their captives in the second century, they forced them to work, making large plantations both possible and profitable. These changes made the Roman Republic a slave-based society.

Slavery built the economy and the Roman Empire would not have been established without the sweat of slaves. The Empire sprawled across the entire Mediterranean region and at times, slaves outnumbered freemen three times over.

Slaves were everywhere and trained for almost every function: road construction, clerks, secretaries, tax agents, actors and prostitutes. Thousands of slaves shackled together were worked to death in silver and gold mines, with men and women 'half naked . . . in chains, under the lash and guarded by soldiers'. Gladiators performed for public entertainment, fighting to the death. Since slaves outnumbered their owners, there were several revolts, the most famous rebellion led by Spartacus. His force of 90,000 slaves defeated two Roman armies before they were crushed, and 6,000 slave warriors were crucified along the road from Rome to Capua.

In the third century, personal freedom was surrendered for the empowerment of the state; occupations and professions became hereditary, similar to the caste system for the Dalits in India. The labourers on agricultural estates emerged as *coloni*, or tenant farmers, whose labour repaid their debt.

Romans themselves did not learn practical skills and relied heavily on their slaves for most services in agriculture, government and home life. Some historians think that this attitude contributed to the downfall of the Roman Empire.

How the early church dealt with slaves

The Christian scriptures did not explicitly advocate the abolition of slavery, but did give instructions on how slaves should be treated. Slavery in the Bible differed from present-day concepts and was not based on race or ethnicity, but was more to do with social status. A Hebrew debt slave was limited to six years (Exodus 21:2; Deuteronomy 15:12); when a slave was freed, he received gifts that enabled him to survive economically (Deuteronomy 15:14).

Slaves who converted to Christianity found encouragement in the theme of Hebrew liberation and the promise of a homeland, the calls for justice by the prophets, and the teachings of Jesus, who identified with the poor and marginalised. All spoke to their experience of bondage and oppression.

But the implications were clear. In the first century, the apostle Paul wrote, 'In him, the distinctions between Jew and Greek, slave and freeman, male and female, disappear; you are all one in

Christ' (Galatians 3:28). This was a dynamic and revolutionary message demonstrating God's compassion towards individuals, and would have been of great appeal to the slave population.

As both slaves and slave owners came to personal faith, it created a dynamic tension within the Christian community. The apostle Paul wrote to the church in Colossae, 'Slaves, obey those who are your masters on earth' (Colossians 3:22). To the slave owners he said, 'Masters, grant your slaves justice and fairness' (Colossians 4:1).

When a runaway slave, Onesimus, became a Christian, Paul wrote to his master, Philemon, another believer, and entrusted the young convert with the letter. He instructed the slave owner to treat his slave kindly or to liberate him.

Early church leaders, including Ovidivus, Chromatius and Hermes, freed their slaves and anyone joining the ministry became free automatically. Two years after the Emperor Constantine legalised Christianity, he imposed the death penalty on anyone stealing children to be raised as slaves. In the sixth century, the Christian Emperor Justinian ordered the death penalty for anyone who raped a female slave.

The church exercised huge political power and with Christianity the official religion of the Roman Empire, its message spread across Europe and the Middle East.

The institution of slavery was accepted by the early church leaders, who advocated better treatment for slaves and the release of captives. It was resignation rather than abolition. The full implications of Paul's words were not explored further, although as the Christian message spread, slavery declined.

THE ANGLES

When Pope Gregory saw blond slaves in a slave market in Rome, he was told they were Angles. 'Not Angles but angels,' he replied, and sent St Augustine to convert the Anglo-Saxons.

This legend was handed down by the Venerable Bede, a monk in Jarrow, born around 672, who first articulated the idea of one English nation in 732. Ethelbert was the first king in England, with his kingdom of Kent, to accept the Christian faith.

How slavery evolved in Europe

With the fall of the Roman Empire, several Germanic kingdoms moved across the conquered land.

The Franks and the Burgundians invaded Gaul and their kingdom became modern France. The Longbeards took Italy. The Goths and Vandals marched as far as Spain. Britain was overrun by three tribes, the Angles, Saxons and Jutes.

The invading barbarians spread their own tribal customs, beliefs and institutions, and their particular brand of slavery. In time, slavery turned into the system known as serfdom, a legal status for peasant labourers forced to work their land for wealthy privileged landowners, who thought that they had a fundamental right to exploit the labour of the poor and that it was acceptable to own slaves. Europe was moving back to the influence of Aristotle. The masters in France, Germany and elsewhere had land with inanimate tools – plough, harrow, sickle and hoe – and now the serfs became part of the property. It was this idea that provided the philosophical justification for the institution of slavery that was passed on through the generations.

Germany's conflict with her neighbours, the Slavs, from the eighth to the tenth century, provided a constant supply of prisoners of war. Eventually all captives, regardless of race, were known as Slavs, giving us the very word 'slave'.

In post-Roman Britain, Celtic descendants clung to their ancient culture in remote areas, where farming was primitive, unlike other agricultural regions, where a larger slave labour force was needed. It was into this landscape that the Anglo-Saxons (the English) carried their own form of slavery, and their laws gave some protection to slaves. The Danes occupying eastern England enslaved people, and the Domesday Book, listing all the farms in the kingdom, showed that slaves numbered about 10 per cent of the population.

Serfdom was another step towards slavery, but a sense of freedom emerged when King John signed the Magna Carta in 1215, the most important legal document in the history of democracy.

In England the serfs were enslaved after the eleventh century, but the feudal system was ending and unfair taxes provoked a young priest to fight the unjust system. John Wycliffe did this by translating the Bible into English, and for the first time the oppressed peasants heard that God had ordained all people to be free. But the state was unrelenting, and in the sixteenth century a law was passed that serfs who left their farms should be branded on their forehead with the letter 'S'.

Wycliffe's campaign was eventually successful and the oppression of the serfs ended when Queen Elizabeth granted freedom to all in her kingdom.

Historians have declared that it is mathematically certain that almost every English person has more than one serf or villein in his or her lineage.

Scotland liberated serfs early, but revived a form of chattel slavery in 1606, forcing coal and salt miners to continue their work. Iron collars were riveted around their necks and they could be bought and sold as part of the mine installations.

In Europe serfdom eventually declined, except in Russia, where as late as 1850 about three quarters of the population were peasants, numbering some 60 million.

By the late fifteenth century, Europe had grown used to the enslavement of people. The church advocated better treatment of slaves, but did not abolish slavery, and as the Christian faith spread, Aristotle's influence made slavery acceptable in the centuries that followed.

The kingdoms of Greece and Rome contributed important foundations such as law, democracy and the apparatus of civilisation in the forms of roads, cities and ports. Its darker legacy was to have a profound and enduring impact: slavery.

The traditional forms of slave serfdom can be told through two English words: 'clown' and 'villain'.

In Roman times, the *colonus* was a free citizen, a soldier-farmer who emigrated across the Roman Empire, recalled today by Cologne (Köln) on the Rhine and Lincoln in England, whose second syllable reveals its origins. When these old soldiers became merely farmers, a *colonus* became a stooped old country bumpkin, a target of jest and contempt, who laboured long hours for his master.

The *villein* in his day was also a man of honour. In the Empire, agricultural industries used slaves alongside freemen, who were labourers known as *villeins* – the men of the villa.

Both *coloni* and *villeins* were compelled to force their children to follow them into servitude, and gradually they lost their freedom or the right to change their vocation. They retained their farms, but their produce went to others.

The rise of Islam

Like other cultures over time, the Arab world traded in slaves. Arab traders settled along the African coast, resulting in the emergence of the Swahili, who served as intermediaries between Africans from the interior and ships from India and China. The Africans exchanged gold and ivory for imported cotton garments, luxury goods and slaves.

The spread of Islam from the eighth century was achieved by Arabs who had conquered North Africa. Islam accepted slavery, and its military expansion saw an increase in prisoners of war and therefore enslaved people. In *The Atlas of Slavery* James Walvin noted, 'From the 8th to the 20th century large numbers of slaves were moved, mainly by foot, across the Sahara to Islamic slave markets dotted around the Mediterranean.'

Although statistics are impossible to confirm, it is possible that the numbers of enslaved Africans taken in this way were similar to the transatlantic slave trade, since the Middle Eastern trade started a millennium before and continued for a century after the Europeans had ended trading.

The BBC's *Story of Africa* reported, 'African slaves ended up as sailors in Persia, pearl divers in the Gulf, soldiers in the Omani army and workers in Mesopotamia, modern Iraq. Many were domestic slaves in rich households. Women were taken as sex slaves.'

Africans were used as eunuchs and Arab traders set up 'eunuch stations' along the major slave routes. The victims were boys aged between 8 and 12 years old, and the survival rate ranged between 1 in 10 and 1 in 30. In ninth-century Baghdad, the Caliph Al-Amin owned about 7,000 black eunuchs and 4,000 white eunuchs.

The Muslims of the Middle East took slaves of all colours and ethnicities, but white slaves, particularly women, were most valuable, and racist attitudes were evident. The Wikipedia encyclopaedia notes, 'Racist opinions recurred in the works of Arab historians and geographers: so in the 14th century Ibn Khaldun could write "The only people to accept slavery without any hope of return are the Negroes, because of an inferior degree of humanity, their place being closer to the animal level."'

The Moors, a Muslim people from Morocco, become Europe's main procurers of all races of slaves by the mid-fifteenth century, with piracy the second.

Arab traders sold about 1,000 African slaves into Europe each year. The German artist Albrecht Dürer sketched an African servant, while the Spanish painter Diego Velazquez acquired a slave who was eventually freed and became a talented artist known as Juan de Pareja.

It was common for both Christian and Muslim groups to enslave each other; it has been estimated that North African Muslim pirates abducted and enslaved more than one million Europeans between 1530 and 1780. They were seized from Italy, Spain, Portugal, France, Britain, even Iceland, and taken captive in (what is today) Morocco, Tunisia, Algeria and Libya. These white slaves were put to work in quarries, building sites and galleys, and female slaves were caged in palace harems; others were held hostage and bargained for ransom. Miguel de Cervantes was captured by Barbary pirates and enslaved in Algeria. He tried to escape several times, but was finally ransomed by his family after five years. Years after his release, he became known as the author of *Don Quixote*.

Today, barely any remnant remains of an African population in Arab lands. It is hardly surprising, with a high death rate and low birth rate, since males were castrated.

Between the ninth and fifteenth centuries, other slave-based societies rose and fell in Africa. Just as in other parts of the world, the practice of slavery varied from culture to culture, although there was no great demand for slave labour at the time.

Dramatic changes were about to happen, however, as Europe started to colonise its new world discoveries. African kingdoms turned from the desert to the sea for trade with the coming of the Europeans.

Slavery in Africa

In Africa, slavery had a social and cultural context which imposed definition and restraint on the master and his slave.

The BBC noted that many African societies with kings and hierarchical forms of government traditionally kept slaves. These were mostly used for domestic purposes, and were an indication of power, wealth and status, and not used for commercial gain. African slavery dealt with prisoners of war, debtors and criminals, and most remained in a culture similar to their own. After 1650, the need for a labour force for overseas plantations had a transforming effect within Africa, and as the demand increased, this gave way to kidnapping and capture in armed raids on neighbouring villages.

James Walvin, in *The Atlas of Slavery*, observed that Europeans had known about African slaves long before the development of the Americas. 'Islamic overland slave systems had delivered

Africans to the slave markets of southern Europe and the eastern Mediterranean (and elsewhere). It was the very existence of Islamic slave routes within Africa that first alerted Europeans to the possibilities of acquiring and developing their own slave trading systems.'

Africans and Europeans had a different concept of wealth. In Europe, an individual could own land and any wealth it could produce. In Africa, the opposite was true. Land was available to anyone who could secure the labour to clear it, and a man's wealth was decided not by the size of the property, but by the quantity of food it supplied. Private ownership of labour rather than land increased their security and wealth, and therefore family members, dependants and slaves were beneficial. In Europe a landowner was taxed on land, but in Africa it was bodies.

Issues over 'Africans enslaving Africans' are contradictory. The concept of an 'African' was invented by Europeans, and had no meaning for Africans during the transatlantic slave trade. Africans had no common identity or sense of 'being African', but were comprised of different peoples, nations, clans, languages and ethnic groups. When trading slaves, they were trading a different nation from themselves. Each people group was as different as a Cockney would be to a Basque or a Cornishman, Bavarian, Breton, Frisian, Gorani, Lipovan or the Boyko and Lemkos, the mountain people of Central Europe.

SLAVERY NOW – AND THEN

How the transatlantic slave trade developed

How did the slave trade start?

The transatlantic slave trade was the largest international business of the time, and it launched a new world order.

During the fifteenth and sixteenth centuries, Europe, Africa and the Americas came together to create new societies and economies. Slavery was central to that new world history, as slaves provided the labour force that drove this new international financial system. After that, no one was untouched by the institution of slavery, and it is central to an understanding of our world today.

Transatlantic slavery transformed the world beyond anything anyone could ever comprehend. But how did it start?

There have always been slaves, but the transatlantic slave trade was different.

And the world at the time was different. Mysterious and enticing. Who knew what lay beyond the horizon? Riches. Fame. Power.

The main reasons for people moving around the world during the fifteenth and sixteenth centuries was exploration and trade. Seamen and mariners were searching for a way to the East. Explorers wanted to find a direct route to India and China. This discovery would bring treasures and rewards. Adventurers lay awake at night dreaming of discovering secret passages into the deep unknown. Emperors were anxious to conquer new worlds and maintain their power and influence.

The search for gold became a major driving force that compelled buccaneers to grow restless.

Gold took on significance in the eleventh and twelfth centuries, when first the Muslim countries of the Mediterranean and then several European ones adopted that metal as their currency. In the late Middle Ages, Europe's main source of gold was in West Africa.

Africa's riches were legendary, coveted by all, and stories such as that of Mansa Musa held everyone spellbound. The Muslim ruler of Mali had given away so much gold on a trip to Cairo that the metal became devalued. For centuries afterwards, his image appeared on maps of the world as a symbol of Africa's immense treasures. In ancient Ghana, gold was so plentiful that it had to be restricted to hold its value.

Many of Europe's luxuries came from the Far East and Africa, brought by Muslim traders. Portugal was impressed with the size and quantity of African ivory and the intricate workmanship of the African artisans. If only they could trade directly with Africa . . .

The Moors controlled the trade routes, and North Africa had become a battleground between Christians and Muslims. If the sea could be conquered, they could sail around the hostile forces and trade directly with the people who produced the products they wanted.

There were other reasons. Portugal was a Christian country, and they were keen to spread their faith.

African slaves were highly valued by the Portuguese, who were the first to use them in their colony of Madeira, off the west coast of Morocco, in 1444. The Portuguese had grown sugar with tremendous success and it created a sensation. The plantations needed a workforce, and at first slaves from Russia and the

Balkans produced the lucrative commodity. But this labour supply was cut off when the Turks captured Constantinople, closing off that route. At the time, Africans were seen as replacements for Eastern European slaves and were sold by Arab traders, who purchased them directly from Africa.

Over the next five decades, two significant events were to change the course of world history for ever.

First, Portugal opened up the west coast of Africa. Second, Columbus 'discovered' America.

These landmarks happened within 50 years of each other. Interestingly, both Spain and Portugal were Christian countries where slavery was an accepted practice.

The first to reach Africa

Prince Henry of Portugal's reputation as a visionary was enhanced by his school for cartographers, explorers and ship's pilots called The House of Winds. He urged his mariners to discover a direct route to the Orient by finding a new pathway across the sea.

The first Portuguese ships touched the coast of Africa in 1435, proving that such journeys could be accomplished. Africans on the coastline had never seen such an unusual craft on the sea and the Europeans grabbed the inquisitive ones who got too close to the unidentified sailing object. In 1444, a few hundred men, women and children were kidnapped from the African coast, baptised when they returned to Portugal, and then sold by public auction that summer.

The Portuguese mariners realised that locating a direct source of slave labour for their colonies meant that they did not have to rely on Arab traders. Official diplomatic missions opened trade relations with West African states, and by the time of Prince Henry's death in 1460, about 1,000 African slaves were being imported annually. His enterprise placed Portugal as the leading nation in the known world.

Why Africans became the most popular slaves

After news of Portugal's discoveries spread across Europe, the King and Queen of Spain decided to fund an enthusiastic explorer to take to the sea. At the time, some accepted facts determined the action of all. The sun revolved around the earth. The world was flat. If you sailed into the horizon, you would fall off the edge.

But not everyone agreed. One young adventurer was sure the earth was a globe. A sailor since the age of 14, he hawked his ideas around, seeking a benefactor to fund his expedition. He was sure he was right. He was sure he could discover the route to the Far East. He was sure he could discover gold. All he needed was someone to believe in him. Someone with a lot of money. But everyone, including Henry VII of England, refused.

Twenty years later, support finally came from the Spanish royal family, who decided to take a chance on plans that the 41-year-old Christopher Columbus laid before them.

Columbus sailed west in search of a route to Asia and, thinking he had reached the East Indies, he landed on an island which he named San Salvador – the Isle of the Holy Saviour. He sailed on to Cuba and to Haiti, which he named Hispaniola – Little Spain. Instead of reaching the coveted East Indies, however, he discovered the West Indies and the Americas.

Although frustrated that he had not detected gold, and determined to show the benefits of his expedition, he sent back a few captured Native Taino Indians to be sold in Spanish slave markets. This was the first known cargo of slaves to cross the Atlantic.

More Native Indians followed, as Columbus planned to send 4,000 slaves a year for sale in Spain. He had worked out that an investment of 3,000,000 *maravedis* would bring in a profit of 17,000,000 *maravedis* when the slaves were sold in Europe.

Queen Isabella stopped the sale, believing that these natives were her new subjects, not foreigners, and could not be exploited in this way.

But the Queen's ruling was to be ignored as Spanish conquistadors surged through the unexplored world in search of hidden treasures.

As the Spanish expanded their realm, they set up colonies, appointed governors and created an infrastructure that could manage the new businesses. The expanding European empires lacked one major resource: a workforce. At first, the Native Indians were commanded to work. If anyone remembered the Queen's edict, no one said anything.

The pace of events was astonishing.

Eight years after Columbus's first journey, the Atlantic had become a known ocean, crossed and recrossed by numerous ships, revolutionising travel and trade. Spanish investments were paying off, and soon wealth was starting to flow from the new world to the old.

But there was trouble in Paradise.

The desire for gold intensified. The Spanish conquistadors dreamed of great gold mines in which the hard work would be done by the Indians. But the indigenous population were not used to the back-breaking labour, and they died from overwork, grief and modern diseases such as smallpox and measles. Indian resistance was extinguished by the Spaniards' superior firepower, and massacres followed.

To solve the problem, white and black slaves were bought in Spain's slave markets, baptised and shipped out. White indentured servants were tried, but proved a failure. Desperately seeking slaves, some turned to kidnapping naive youth, particularly in England, where Bristol became dangerous territory for the young and gullible.

In Hispaniola, the native population had been reduced from an estimated 3 million in 1494 to just 25,000 who were able to work in 1510. By 1520 the indigenous inhabitants in the Caribbean had almost vanished.

The solution to the crisis caused Spain to turn to Africa. The African slaves had distinguished themselves. They came from more advanced societies, could grow crops in tropical conditions, were skilled craftsmen, knew how to domesticate animals and were immune to European diseases. And they were hard workers. A dispatch to the King of Spain reported that the work of one black slave equalled that of four Indians. Diego Colon, Columbus's son, explained that the Indians found the gold mines hard work – they struggled 'to break the rocks in which the gold is found'.

In 1510, eleven years after Columbus's first voyage and while he was still alive, the King authorised the first shipload of African slaves to be sent from Lisbon to work alongside the Indians. The slaves were purchased from slave markets in Spain and did not come directly from Africa.

In 1518, the Spanish government made the enslavement of Indians illegal, and that same year a contract was issued to a Flemish merchant authorising him to deliver 4,000 slaves annually to Spanish colonies directly from Africa. African slaves were in such demand that the merchant was able to sell his contract and turn a profit.

In Brazil, the Portuguese faced a similar problem and reached the same conclusion as the Spanish. They had to have slaves. They had to come from Africa.

For the first time, it was the continent of Africa that was to supply all the slaves needed for the new enterprises of the Europeans.

In simple terms, the transatlantic slave trade started because the Native Americans did not make good slaves.

Over the next four centuries, between 9 and 15 million slaves were stolen and shipped as slaves in 54,000 slave voyages to service an international business enterprise that expanded the economies of all slave-trading nations. Essentially, the slaves of Africa developed European nations and contributed to their wealth and success.

Slavery was the key to the making of the modern world.

SLAVERY NOW – AND THEN

Hatuey's stand

An epic struggle ensued in Cuba in 1512. Hatuey, the Indian chief, was defeated by the superior weapons of the Spanish and, according to *Black History: Slavery*, an explorer recorded the following conversation between Hatuey and a Spanish priest.

Priest: Will you accept Christianity before you die?

Hatuey: Why?

Priest: So that you may go to Heaven, son.

Hatuey: Do Christians go to Heaven?

Priest: Yes, if they die in the grace of God.

Hatuey: If the Christians go to Heaven, I do not want to go to Heaven. I do not wish ever again to meet such cruel and wicked people, as Christians, who kill and make slaves of the Indians.

The bishop's 'solution'

The Bishop of Chiapas was distressed at the plight of the aboriginal people and he returned to Spain to petition the king on their behalf. The bishop knew that he had to be pragmatic if he was to be successful, and proposed a solution: slaves from Africa. Hugh Thomas noted in *The Slave Trade*, 'Like all enlightened men of his time, he believed that an African enslaved by Christians was more fortunate than an African in domestic circumstances.' Later, he realised that it was wrong to replace one form of slavery for another, but this was not published for several years.

The achievement of Columbus

At the time, the Western hemisphere was a place apart and played no role in the economic life of Europe, Asia or Africa. Today, America is the centre of the world economy and for many the symbol of twenty-first-century globalisation.

Columbus's 'discovery' revolutionised international trade and sparked an explosion in travel and global trade, but it also led to the greatest forced migration in history – and the boom in slavery.

England starts late, finishes first

Spain and Portugal were the superpowers of the age and led the world in exploration and discovery. They assumed they could control the Atlantic Ocean, the key to future prosperity. But there was fierce rivalry between both nations, and the Pope's intervention was necessary to calm the tension between these loyal Catholic countries. The competition was settled as they carved up the known world.

Portugal claimed land to the east, which included Brazil, and Spain got most of Columbus's recently discovered new worlds. According to the deal, only Portugal could trade with Africa. At times, the monopoly cranked up the pressure, when Portugal refused Spain access to African slaves.

In England, an enterprising John Hawkins spotted a business opportunity. Seeking fame and fortune, he sailed with three ships from Plymouth in 1562.

Hawkins seized some 300 Africans in Sierra Leone, 'by the sword and partly by other means', and sold his cargo to the Spanish West Indies. It was England's first entry into the slave trade, although Hawkins's father had been the first Englishman to touch the African shore 30 years earlier.

Hawkins was the first Englishman to take up the slave trade as a serious business. His trip was so profitable that he returned a second time, and his backers included Queen Elizabeth I, who provided a royal ship, *Jesus of Lubeck*, for the journey. By the time she ascended to the throne, hundreds of English subjects had been captured, sold to Arab masters and enslaved in North Africa. She expressed the hope to Hawkins that Africans would not be enslaved without first giving their consent.

The plantation owners in the Caribbean needed new slaves and they welcomed Hawkins. The Devon adventurer returned home with tropical produce such as sugar, ginger, pearls, hides and, for the first time, tobacco and the potato. Hawkins produced a 60 per cent profit on the investment and received a hero's welcome.

Although he committed treason, murder and adultery at various times in his career, he was knighted in 1588 for his role in defeating the Spanish Armada.

His third journey in 1567, with a young Francis Drake on board, proved a disaster.

He helped the King of Sierra Leone to storm a fortified town and was rewarded with 500 captives. It is interesting to learn how they were selected. His allies 'drove seven thousand Negroes into the sea at low tide, at the point of land, where they were all drowned in the ooze except for five hundred which we took and carried thence for traffic to the West Indies'. But Hawkins's vessels were ambushed by a Spanish fleet, which captured the Queen's ships in Mexico; Hawkins and Drake narrowly escaped death.

Portugal and Spain accused Hawkins of 'piracy' and the skirmish eventually led to a confrontation in the English Channel in 1588. Spanish mastery of the seas ended abruptly with the defeat of its Armada at the hands of the English navy. Spain's position as the world's leading sea power was destroyed.

With ships now free to sail the Atlantic, Spain's grip on its overseas territory loosened. The new lands conquered by Spain and Portugal had proved enticing and as news spread of potential wealth, other nations were determined to cut themselves a slice of the profits.

The desire for more land and an economy based on profit became the driving force that defined most decisions. Backed by wealthy investors, European countries exploited the natural and mineral resources of the new territories in the Americas and the Caribbean.

But the gold and silver mines and the plantations required manual labour. Again, African slaves became highly prized commodities.

It seemed as though everyone was on the move, and the Spanish and Portuguese faced challenges from the Dutch, French, Swedes, Danes and Brandenburgers. The English were late starters.

Hawkins's last enterprise may have been a disaster, but English businessmen were convinced that there was a profit to be made in the slaving industry. Their logic was indisputable. Everyone else was getting rich from it.

In 1663, King Charles II granted a charter to the Royal Adventurers into Africa, and to celebrate the venture a new coin was minted from pure African gold. It was named the guinea, in recognition of the coast of Guinea, virtually the whole of West Africa. It declared to the world that the African coast that had enriched other European nations was now England's hunting ground as well. The corporation traded in gold, African goods and enslaved people, and in 1665 it was estimated that the company earned £100,000 from trading slaves. The corporation was funded by seven knights of the realm, four barons, five earls, a marquis, two dukes and four members of the royal family.

Despite fierce rivalry and setbacks, English patrons were determined to grab some of the business that was enriching European nations, and a new corporation was set up. The Royal African Company, with James, Duke of York, as its governor and largest shareholder, ensured that London became the largest slaving port in Britain, and the city provided the finance for all the slave voyages.

Over the next 20 years, the shareholders of the corporation were delighted with the profits from the trade in gold, spices and slaves. King Charles gave the company exclusive rights of trade, but in 1697, under pressure from piracy and other traders, the business was opened to all English ships, in return for 10 per cent of the cargo's value. By 1713 the corporation had built eight forts on the African coast, transported 120,000 slaves to the Americas and imported 30,000 tons of sugar from the West Indies. By the end of the seventeenth century, as much as three fifths of the RAC's income came from the sale of slaves, the balance from gold, gum and other products.

In 1713 Britain won the contract to provide slaves to Spanish colonies in the Americas, and the government sold the privilege to the South Sea Company for £7.5 million. The corporation was plagued with difficulties and collapsed a few years later. One successful investor, the London bookseller Thomas Guy, had sold his shares as they peaked. He used his massive fortune to establish Guy's Hospital for 'the poorest and sickest of the poor' in London.

During the eighteenth century, traders bought their slaves for between £2 and £3 each, and when sold, could multiply their investment by nearly 20 per cent. With the proceeds they purchased sugar, cotton, rum and tobacco, which were sold for even more profit in England.

Business was booming.

What was Africa like before the slave trade?

At the start of the fifteenth century, Africa and the developed area of Western Europe were considered equal by the first foreigners to reach West Africa. Peaceworks reported, 'The University of Timbuktu was as old as the University of Paris and attracted scholars from across West Africa and the Maghreb.' Africa had huge reserves of natural wealth, while Europe was distinguished by its lack of reserves. The people of West Africa were an advanced civilisation. Most of them were farmers who had experience of growing crops in tropical conditions. Others were hunters and fishermen, or skilled craftsmen such as ironworkers, miners and carpenters. They had their own religion, music and art. Communities lived in large family units around a central palace. The slaves from this area were so valuable that they were called 'black gold'.

John Wesley wrote of the Ivory Coast in 1774,

> The soil is fertile, producing abundance of rice and roots. Indigo and cotton thrive without cultivation; fish is in great plenty; the flocks and herds are numerous, the trees laden with fruit. [The land] . . . is exceedingly fruitful and pleasant, producing vast quantities of rice and other grain, plenty of fruit and roots, palm wine and oil, fish in great abundance, with tame and wild cattle. It is one of the most fruitful, most pleasant countries in the known world. It is said to be unhealthy; and so it is to strangers, but perfectly healthy to the native inhabitants.

The interior of Africa was a mass of nations, kingdoms, empires and tribes, with towns and villages linked by trade routes.

The city of Benin was one of the largest in the world during the sixteenth and seventeenth centuries, with art, culture and nobility comparable to many European cities and surpassing others. A Dutch businessman who visited Benin for the first time was impressed with its remarkable architecture, thriving commerce and industry. He wrote of 'great broad streets, seven or eight times broader than Warmoes Street in Amsterdam, which goes right out and never bends. The houses in this town stand in good order, one close and even with the other, as the houses in Holland stand.'

Benin and the Congo were major kingdoms with centralised seats of power and forms of government and organisation similar to foreign systems.

The structure of many societies focused around the king; below him were pyramids of authority based on kinship. They had seen the rise and fall of large empires throughout their history. African society was governed by established laws and traditions, and Arab traders had noted that they could travel freely without fear of robbery or violence. Prisoners of war were treated as individuals with limited rights. As the slave trade increased, the concept of an economic value for labour emerged, and more powerful members of society came to view their dependants and captives not by their class and hierarchy, but by their worth.

The king of the Congo was the first West African ruler to convert to Christianity at the turn of the fifteenth century, and several African noblemen were educated in Europe. The British government tried to gain favour with important Africans by inviting their sons to England to learn the language.

Most African languages had never gained a written form, so there was no literature or history and they relied on an oral tradition.

Much of Africa's indigenous arts and crafts did not survive war, climate and colonisation, but many African treasures are housed in the British Museum and similar establishments.

How the trade impacted Africa

In most cultures, traditions define our morals, and anything acceptable is right.

For centuries, African tribes and kingdoms had practised selected forms of slavery, and they had a long tradition of selling their prisoners of war and criminals, first to Arab traders and later to Europeans with ships.

As the transatlantic slave trade increased, the demand for more slaves put pressure on African tribal leaders to supply human cargo, so urgently needed for the commodities of the new world.

When a prince from the Congo region was captured, the Sonyo people refused to trade with the Dutch. He was located and returned with apologies.

In 1726, the King of Dahomey (modern Benin) suggested that Europeans should establish plantations in his kingdom. He would supply the slaves.

The coastal rulers who co-operated with the Europeans grew wealthy and extended their influence into the interior. The growth of the slave trade strengthened states such as Dahomey, but Benin avoided the trade for a time and also matured as a state. Hugh Thomas observed that the slave trade must have encouraged African monarchies not just to go to war, but to capture more prisoners than before. He noted, 'A few African rulers tried to escape from participation in the transatlantic trade. Mostly, they failed. All were caught up in a vast scheme of things which seemed normal at least until 1780.'

BUYERS CREATE SELLERS

Ottobah Cugoana, a freed Fanti slave who published his memoirs in 1787, was kidnapped as a child and sold 'at a European fort for one gun, one piece of cloth and a small quantity of lead'. He was 'first kidnapped and betrayed by my own complexion, who were the first cause of my exile and slavery', but, he added, 'if there were no buyers, there would be no sellers'.

How the trade operated

It was called a triangular route: the first voyage from Europe to Africa shipped goods to trade; the second from Africa to the Americas carried human cargo; the third from the Americas back to Europe took colonial produce.

Changes in ship design in the fifteenth century made long journeys across the ocean possible. The first change was the invention of the stern rudder, improving the steering; the second was the replacement of one big sail by three masts and many sails, which made the ship easier to handle.

In 1787, one ship's cargo included guns, powder, shot, lead and iron pots, pewter basins, copper kettles and pans, iron, silver and gold rings, lengths of cotton and linen, silk handkerchiefs, beads, scarlet cloth, coarse blue and red woollen cloths, coarse and fine hats, worsted caps, spirits and tobacco.

The journey from Africa to America was the longest and could take two to three months. Ships carried anything from 250 to 600 slaves, in terrible conditions, and about 20 per cent of slaves were thought to have died in transit. According to the BBC, although all figures were recorded, documents that revealed the number of losses have disappeared.

The business of slavery

The capture of Olaudah Equiano

At times, it felt like a game. The boy hides in a tree, quite still, only his imagination runs wild. But this was no childish entertainment of hide-and-seek. He had to remain vigilant, alert to strangers in the village, kidnappers who would seize and carry them off as slaves.

On that day, the ten-year-old boy spotted a man acting suspiciously, and raised the alarm. Other children were the first at the scene. They pinned the prowler down and restrained him with ropes.

His father was some distance away with the other adults from the village, cultivating a farm. When he returned home and heard the news, he praised his son. Everyone in the community knew that the slave trade made life dangerous and violent.

Olaudah Equiano's father was one of the village elders, many of whom were like magistrates. He lived in an estate, consisting of many houses made from the soil's hard red earth, inside a boundary wall. The biggest abode stood in the centre of the compound, and the other one-storey thatched buildings circled it.

The men and women in Equiano's village dressed alike, in a kind of sarong or kilt, made in the village from cotton material, dyed bright blue with the juice from wild berries.

Everyone in the village had a role. When the women stayed at home and prepared the meals, it was usually stewed beef, goat or chicken, flavoured with pepper and a kind of salt made from wood ash. Vegetables were beans, sweetcorn, a starchy root called yam, and a type of banana called plantain. Palm trees provided oil and nuts and, for the adults, palm wine.

Equiano's father was a man of position and, in keeping with African custom, he owned slaves, but they were included in community life, treated fairly and shared responsibilities within the village.

The boy looked forward to market days, when he walked to the town square with his mother, accompanied sometimes by his brothers and sister. The villagers sold salt and sweet-smelling wood in exchange for beads and dried fish, quite a luxury since there were no lakes or large rivers nearby. Sometimes there would be men from down south, slave traders who brought slaves to the town square to sell. They would entice his father or the village chiefs to sell slaves in exchange for foreign-made muskets or sparkling trinkets. In keeping with tradition, only criminals or prisoners of war would be sold.

Another day, Equiano was left at home with his older sister, while all the adults were away. This time, someone else was on lookout.

They never heard the intruders, but two men and a woman quietly climbed over the wall, skulking around.

It happened in a flash. When they realised the danger, it was too late. Equiano and his sister were seized and gagged, and their abductors dragged them into the dense woods.

Years later, he wrote one of the most influential books on the slave trade and recalled that the incident that was to change his life for ever was over in a minute. It 'put an end to all my happiness'.

With their hands tied, the boy and his sister walked through the woods. On the second day they saw travellers, but before he could call out to them, Equiano was gagged again, and he was placed in a sack until they had passed by. The next day, another heartbreak. He was separated from his sister, who was sold to another gang of kidnappers. It was the last time he saw her.

Equiano was sold, and sold again, with the price increasing each time. Although he did not know it, he was moving nearer the coast. He recalled,

> I was carried to the left of the sun's rising through many different countries and a number of large woods. The people I was sold to carried me when I was tired, either on their shoulders or on their back. All the nations and people that I had hitherto passed through, resembled our own in their manner, customs and language, but I came to a country that differed from us . . . I continued to travel, sometimes by land, sometimes by water, through different countries and various nations, till at the end of six or seven months after I had been kidnapped, I arrived at the sea coast.

The child was exhausted by the time the kidnappers and their slaves reached the shore. It was there that he caught sight of the ocean for the first time in his life. But he was intrigued by another mystifying object. Anchored near the water's edge, gently swaying in the cool breeze, its anchor ropes creaking slightly, was a structure he had never seen before: a ship.

The selling of Olaudah Equiano

Olaudah Equiano was born in 1745, an Ibo from the Eboe region of modern Nigeria. Africans who were kidnapped or sold were chained and forced to march to the coast, sometimes as far as 1,000 miles. At the coast, European traders and corporations such as King Charles II's Royal Adventurers had set up forts and trading posts, and their representatives waited for the latest merchandise to arrive. Sometimes the slaves would have to wait in 'barracoons' or stockades until a ship sailed in and a deal was completed.

The ritual never altered. Stripped naked, head shaved, they would undergo a physical examination to ensure good health, with special attention paid to their teeth, telltale signs of age. It was common for a sailor to lick the sweat of an African, thinking that its taste could tell if they were ill. The Portuguese baptised their slaves before they left African soil. Finally, a hot branding iron burned the corporation's name on their breast or arm so that dealers could identify their merchandise.

It was a traumatic experience for each African man, woman and child. Their final point on African homeland was to pass through the narrow 'door of no return' and step into canoes to be taken on board the ship by sailors. Some thought the strange white men were cannibals, and fainted from fright and shock. Men were shackled in pairs, wrist to wrist, ankle to ankle. Chained together, they hobbled forward; down they stumbled, into the hold of the ship. It was a descent into a living hell.

Every African left behind his or her name, family, home, language, identity, country and tradition. For anyone who survived, it was Year Zero.

The Middle Passage

The second part of the triangular trade was called the Middle Passage. It was the journey from Africa to the Americas and the Caribbean. Slavers packed between 250 and 600 Africans into the space between the cargo hold and the lower deck. The hold itself was tiny, and in many ships they were stacked like spoons, with no room to stand up, turn or move.

The *Brookes* was a Liverpool vessel of 320 tons, a typical slave ship of the time, which sometimes carried at least 600 slaves. When measured in Liverpool in 1788, each slave was allocated a space six feet long by sixteen inches wide, and about two and a half feet high. Crowded together, they were usually forced to lie on their backs with their heads between the legs of others.

The worst time for crew and slaves was when the ship was pulling away from the African coast. Hugh Thomas recorded the words of Jacques Savary, a businessman in the eighteenth century:

> From the moment that the slaves are embarked, one must put the sails up. The reason is that these slaves have so great a love for their country that they despair when they see that they are leaving it for-

ever; that makes them die of grief, and I have heard merchants say that they died more often before leaving the port than during the voyage. Some throw themselves into the sea, others hit their heads against the ship, others hold their breath to try and smother themselves, others try to die of hunger from not eating.

A Portuguese clergyman noted,

> It is known that in Angola where they carry the prisoners to the ships, those on land weep copiously, horrified and fearful of the violence that is done, seeing that in addition to taking men against their will they treat them very inhumanely on the ships, whence a great number die suffocated by their own stench and from other bad treatment.

The air in the hold was hot and stale, with the stench of sweaty bodies and human waste. Some ships had designated toilet areas; in others, buckets were used. With slaves chained together, reaching the bucket was difficult, and after several weeks at sea the slave ship stank of urine, faeces and vomit. It was said that a slave ship could be smelt before it could be seen.

Dr Alexander Falconbridge, a surgeon who travelled with a slave ship, observed, 'The excessive heat was not the only thing that rendered their situation intolerable. The deck, that is the floor of their rooms, was so covered with the blood and mucus which had proceeded from them in consequence of the flux [dysentery], that it resembled a slaughterhouse.' His brief visit to the hold 'nearly proved fatal to me also . . . I was so overcome with the heat, stench and foul air that I nearly fainted; and it was only with assistance that I could go on deck.'

Slaves packed tight had to lie in each other's urine, faeces and blood. In such cramped quarters, diseases spread quickly, with dysentery and smallpox the chief causes of death. Often, the living were chained to the dead, until the corpses were thrown overboard.

Iron muzzles and whippings were used to control the slaves, although the crew were treated mercilessly as well. Equiano, aged 10, recalled the voyage.

> I was soon put down under the decks, and there I received such a salutation in my nostrils as I had never experienced in my life: so that, with the loathsomeness of the stench, and crying together, I became so sick and low that I was not able to eat, nor had I the least desire to taste anything.
>
> I now wished for my last friend, death, to relieve me; but soon, to my grief, two of the white men offered me vegetables; and on my refusing to eat, one of them held me fast by the hand, and tied my feet, while the other flogged me severely.

Women were separated from the men and moved more freely around the ship. Girls and young women were at the mercy of crude, sex-starved sailors, and on some ships sexual harassment and rape were just one of the cruelties on the voyage. Equiano recorded that girls as young as ten were raped, and a pregnant woman was raped on a ship captained by John Newton. *Liverpool Capital of the Slave Trade* reported, 'It was Captain Marshall on the Liverpool slaver *Black Joke* who flogged a baby to death for refusing food and then forced the child's mother to throw the corpse overboard.'

The slave auction

The agony of the journey ended as the ships reached their destination, but for the slaves a new ordeal awaited.

Plantation owners, dealers and merchants crowded by the quayside as news spread that a slave ship had docked. Posters advertising the sale of slaves were pinned to notice boards.

The sales were called a 'scramble'. The Africans had been scrubbed, their hair glossed with oil, and they were stacked on the deck, unaware that their bodies were the products on sale. Buyers paid a fixed price to the ship's captain and, like runners in a race, were poised at the side of the ship. A starter's pistol was fired and the dealers rushed on board. The buyers would grab and jostle, poke and prod the slaves. Each buyer would circle his purchase with a card or several handkerchiefs tied together to stop another dealer snatching them away.

It was a chaotic scene, a terrifying experience for the Africans.

Sickly slaves were auctioned by candlelight and bidding lasted until an inch of the candle had burnt. Sometimes doctors purchased the frailest, cured them and earned a profit when they were resold. Slaves too ill to be sold were abandoned on the waterfront and left to die.

The plantation owners complained about the 'scramble' process and wanted time to examine the cargo, and sometimes dealers were invited to view the merchandise before the sale started officially. Later the auctions became less brutal, but were still distressing for the Africans. In markets on the waterfront, the buyers were able to inspect the naked slaves closely before making a selection.

When the sale was completed, they would be branded with the company logo, the Royal African Company or the Church of England's seal. Slaves would be branded each time they were sold.

In Brazil dealers preferred slaves from particular African nations, and had a policy of separating national groups to avoid revolts.

In North America, as the slaves were resold throughout their life, their owners ignored any ties they had formed and family members, or married couples, were sold separately. One slave preacher adapted the marriage vows so that couples vowed to love and to cherish 'till death or distance us do part'. Slaves took their names from their masters, and their names changed each time they were bought by a new owner.

In New Orleans slaves were sold on the auction block and taken to sugar and cotton plantations in the American south. In Louisiana the slave population went from 34,660 to over 350,000 in the 50 years before the Civil War. When war broke out, America had about four million slaves. The increase had been natural. *Black History: Slavery* reported, 'Young women were advertised for sale as "good breeding stock".' One slave trader from Virginia boasted that his successful breeding policies enabled him to sell 6,000 slave children a year. As slaves were the property of the plantation owner, the rape of black women by white males was not considered a crime. The children of mixed race were called 'mulattos'.

Slave prices

Payments were made in silver, merchandise or promissory notes, while it was usual to settle accounts with the produce of the islands: sugar, coffee, cotton, indigo.

The cost of slaves rose as the demand increased. Hugh Thomas recorded sale prices in *The Slave Trade* as follows.

- In the 1440s, one horse for 25 or 30 slaves.
- In 1654 the Dutch charged 2,000 pounds of sugar per slave.
- In 1700, £44 for a man, £23 for a boy, £16 for a girl in Barbados.
- In 1800 slaves sold for $90 in Cuba.
- In 1810, $200 each in Brazil.
- In 1850 slaves sold at $360 in the US.
- In 1851 prices of slaves in Mozambique were about $3–$5.
- In 1852 slaves in Cuba sold at £75.
- In 1859 slaves sold in the US at $1,151 for a girl aged 10, $1,705 for a girl with child, and $500 for an old man.
- In 1864 slaves in Cuba sold at $1,250–$1,500.

A mother's pain

Plantation owners used the threat of selling their slave's children as a way of controlling the parents. In *Life of a Slave Girl*, Harriet Jacobs related how her owner, Dr James Norcom, threatened that he would sell her two children unless she became his mistress. Eventually Dr Norcom sold the children, but with the help of a friend she raised the money and employed a white slave trader to buy them for her. She records here the incident when a slave's children were sold in South Carolina.

> I saw a mother lead seven children to the auction block. She knew that some of them would be taken from her; but they took all. The children were sold to a slave-trader, and the mother was bought by a man in her own town. Before night, her children were all far away. She begged the trader to tell her where he intended to take

them; this he refused to do. How could he, when he knew he would sell them, one by one, wherever he could command the highest price? I met another mother in the street, and her wild, haggard face lives today in my mind. She wrung her hands in anguish, and exclaimed, 'Gone! All gone! Why don't God kill me?' Slavery is terrible for men; but it is far more terrible for women.

A son's loss

Frederick Douglas was born in Maryland in 1817, escaped to New York at the age of 21 and wrote the influential book *Narrative of an American Slave*. He never knew his father and was separated from his mother, whom he saw occasionally. He was under seven years old when he went to work on the plantation, but was treated unkindly by another slave woman. One night, when he was forced to go to bed hungry, the door opened.

I was too hungry to sleep, when who but my own dear mother should come in. She read Aunt Katy a lecture, which was never forgotten. That night I learned as I had never learned before, that I was not only a child, but somebody's child. My mother had walked twelve miles to see me, and had the same distance to travel over before the morning sunrise. I do not remember seeing her again.

The product that transformed the slave trade

Over four centuries, millions of Africans were forced into a ritual of servitude and suffering in countries far from their own. They were never to return home or see their families again. Their world became an endless monotony of gruelling service as day followed day. It was the only life they knew.

In the seventeenth century, the demand for slave workers intensified. A new crop on West Indian plantations caused the change as sugar transformed the slavery business. Nearly two thirds of all slaves captured in the eighteenth century went to work on sugar plantations in the Americas and the Caribbean.

Sugar cane was a crop originally brought from India via Egypt to Cyprus in the tenth century, and was taken to the Americas by Columbus on his second voyage in 1493.

The earliest plantations were set up by the Portuguese on the island of Madeira in 1452 and for the first time, African slaves were set to work. Thirty-four years later, the Portuguese developed the concept and took over the uninhabited West African island of Sao Tome, using African slaves to work their new sugar plantations. Just 19 years later, in 1505, the first sugar cane was grown in Santo Domingo (the modern Dominican Republic). Sugar production in Brazil began almost immediately after the first Portuguese colonies arrived in 1532. In *The Atlas of Slavery*, James Walvin noted, 'The technology, finance and skills of sugar cultivation long perfected in the Mediterranean were now transferred to the Atlantic islands and the sugar shipped direct to North Europe.'

In the sixteenth century, a pound of sugar in Britain cost the equivalent of two days' wages for a labourer. The craze for sweetened tea, coffee and chocolate was sensational and by the seventeenth century, the sugar mill was the largest industrial complex known to modern agriculture. Sugar was the biggest product of the West Indies, and plantation owners made fortunes.

Sugar was essential for the growth of Europe, and helped to pay for Britain's development during the Industrial Revolution. The price of sugar fell, placing it within the reach of the poorer classes in England, and sugar consumption rose by 2,500 per cent over 150 years, as it became affordable to all. This would have been impossible without slavery.

More slaves went to work in Brazil than anywhere else. By the 1630s Brazilian sugar exports dominated the European market, and according to James Walvin, Brazil produced ten times as much sugar as any other colony. As elsewhere, African slaves were imported when the indigenous people were unable to cope, but little information survived about the history of slavery in Brazil. In 1891, all records of slavery – the log books of slave ships, custom house records, documents of sales, ownership papers – were officially destroyed to prevent any shame attached to the families of former slaves. Today, the phenomenon of street children is considered to be a legacy of slavery and the inability to integrate former slaves into society.

A typical day at harvest time meant 14 hours of back-breaking work, six days a week, for men, women and children. About one in every three Africans died within three years of working in the Caribbean, but plantation owners in the West Indies were not overly concerned. Their logic: 'It was cheaper to buy than to breed.'

There was a rising demand for slaves in other industries, including coffee, cotton, tobacco, and in the gold and silver mines. In 1524 African slaves were taken to Cuba to work in the gold mines. Slaves were also used at the docks, in factories and in the household, serving as butlers, footmen, cooks and nannies.

The slave populations were kept in line with intimidation and violence, backed by legislation.

In Jamaica, a 1696 law made the killing of a black slave a crime, but only on the second offence. In 1771, the governor of St Domingo was told, 'If some masters abuse their power they must be reproved in secret, so that the slaves may always be kept in the belief that the master can do no wrong in his dealing with them.'

In North America, slaves were given a life sentence. A 1663 Maryland law stated, 'All Negroes or other slaves within the province, all Negroes to be hereafter imported, shall serve for the term of their lives.' A law introduced six years later declared that if a slave died under punishment, it was not a felony. In reply to pressure on the slave trade, Georgia responded in 1818 by imposing a $1,000 fine on anyone who freed a slave.

In 1688, Sir Hans Sloane observed that black slaves in the Caribbean were punished by

nailing them down on the ground with crooked sticks on every limb and applying the fire by degrees from the feet and hands, burning them gradually up to the head, whereby their pains are extravagant. For lesser crimes, chopping off part of the foot with an axe was used . . . for running away they put iron rings of great weights on their ankles or pothooks around their necks, which are iron rings with two long necks riveted to them, or a spur in the mouth. They are whipped till they are raw; some put on their skins pepper and salt to make them smart, at other times their masters will drop melted wax on their skins and use several very exquisite torments.

Slaves were castrated, blown up with gunpowder, or tied up near wasps' or ants' nests. James Pope-Hennessy reported a case from the *Jamaica Gazette* of a 14-year-old girl late for work, who was so 'unmercifully whipped ... that she fell motionlessly to the ground, and was dragged by her heels to the hospital, where she died'. Pregnant women were made to lie face down on the ground with a hole 'dug in the earth to accommodate the unborn child' and then beaten.

For running away, both ears were cut off and one shoulder was branded. The second time, the buttocks were cut off and the other shoulder was branded. The third time, the penalty was death.

'There is nothing that does more to help the growth of these [West Indian] colonies,' the French government stated in 1670, '[than] the trade of Negroes from Guinea to the Islands.'

The world's No 1 slave trader

England entered the slave trade late, but eventually became the largest slaving nation on earth.

Slavery became the centre point of Britain's political economy, and was accepted both socially and culturally. The investors in the slave trade included Queen Anne, King George I, members of the royal family, most members of parliament, including the Speaker, half the House of Lords, the Lord Chancellor, various Lord Mayors, and respected figures such as Sir Isaac Newton, Jonathan Swift and Daniel Defoe. The Church of England, among other churches, supported and directly benefited from the trade; the profit financed churches in England, as shown by records in Lambeth Palace. Clergy such as the Reverend John Braithwaite owned plantations and slaves, and profited personally.

Over a quarter of all Londoners were involved in the business in some form, and Bristol and Liverpool became boom towns as the country was made rich by the business of slavery. Other ports involved included Lancaster, Whitehaven, Portsmouth, Chester, Preston, Poulton-le-Fylde, Plymouth, Exeter, Dartmouth and Glasgow. The plantation system produced England's first millionaire, William Beckford MP, and S. I. Martin, in *Britain's Slave Trade*, estimated that British slave merchants would have made a profit of £12 million from trading slaves from 1630 to 1807.

The wealth that accumulated in Britain was invested in technological developments, speeding up the Industrial Revolution that was to catapult Britain into becoming a superpower.

The development of England's cities is the starting point in understanding how Britain took the lead.

London was England's largest slaving port and the city provided the finance for all the slaving voyages, as ships owned by London merchants dominated the trade. Immersed in the business of slavery were the Bank of England, Lloyds of London and specialist banks such as Barclays, while Barings Bank and the Midland (now HSBC) were founded with profits from the slave trade.

The English colonies in the Caribbean and North America expanded rapidly and their plantations supplied the demand for sugar at home. The slaving journeys were considered by some as a licence to print money.

London had exclusive rights to control the trade, but Bristol merchants lobbied intensely and forced the capital city to share access to the profitable slavery business.

In 1698, Bristol's first (official) slave ship, the *Beginning*, sailed to the African coast, picked up its cargo of slaves and sold them to plantation owners in Jamaica. S. I. Martin noted, 'Bristol cashed in and dominated the slave trade because it could mass-produce large quantities of copper products easily and cheaply. It was this new wealth, from slaves and the sugar they produced, that helped Bristol to take its place as "England's second city".' The

African trade made fortunes for Bristol's businessmen such as the Pinneys and Edward Colston, although present-day monuments do not mention Colston's association with slaving. Slave landmarks in Bristol include the Wills Memorial Building, Bristol University, the Georgian House, Venturer's House and Land-dogger Trow.

Competition for the slave trade was fierce, and by the 1730s Bristol had been overtaken by Liverpool.

Liverpool's charges were much lower, and to avoid paying duty on goods, ships unloaded their cargo on the Isle of Man and then later smuggled it back to the mainland. Bristol was an expensive port to use and harbour difficulties led to delays and overcrowding of ships. By that point, more than copper products were needed and the northern port benefited from Lancashire's cotton trade. More than that, Liverpool's merchants invested heavily in a political lobby determined to protect and promote the town's interest in the trade.

As a result, Liverpool businessmen were able to undercut Bristol's charges and sell slaves more cheaply, and the demand for slaves carried in Liverpool ships rose.

Although Liverpool had illegally supplied slaves to foreign colonies, the first recorded slave voyage was in 1700, when the *Liverpool Merchant* sold 220 slaves to Barbados for £4,239.

The city's fortune depended on the captains of the slave trade. Some have said that they were treated like local heroes and, according to Neil Grant, 'like the members of a cup-winning football team'. Thirty-seven of the 41 members of Liverpool Council in 1787 were involved in some way with the slave business, as too were all 20 mayors who held office between 1787 and 1807. With the exception of William Roscoe (in 1806–7), all Liverpool MPs of the eighteenth and early nineteenth centuries were either slave traders themselves or defenders of the trade in parliament. Many plantation owners lived in London and some were MPs who voted in the House of Commons to support the slave trade.

To maintain control, parliament passed navigational laws,

SLAVERY NOW – AND THEN

which insisted that the colonies could only trade with England and all trade had to be carried in English ships.

LIVERPOOL LEADS
By the start of the nineteenth century, Liverpool controlled 60 per cent of Britain's share of the slave trade, and about 40 per cent of the entire European trade.

LIVERPOOL TOBACCO AND SUGAR IMPORTS BETWEEN 1704 AND 1810

Year	Tobacco (tons)	Sugar (tons)
1704	600	760
1711	1,600	1,120
1785	2,500	16,600
1810	8,400	46,000

(Information provided by an archive of The Chambré Hardman Trust.)

How slavery developed in North America

Columbus never landed in North America, although his name will forever be linked with its discovery.

Dutch traders bought the island of Manhattan from Native Americans for trade beads and other goods valued at 60 guilders, or $24. They established Fort Amsterdam on the tip of the island in 1626, but 42 years later the English captured the settlement and renamed it New York, after the Duke of York.

The first slave owners in America were Native American tribes such as the Klamath, Pawnee, Yurok, Creek, Mandan and Comanche, but their captives were usually small numbers and contained within their culture.

The Dutch were important players on the global scene with active interests in the slave trade and several global colonies. They brought the first African slaves to America and sold them, as indentured servants, in Virginia in 1619.

English settlers arrived in the *Mayflower* in 1620 and set up plantations, but their experiment of using European labourers failed. Like everyone else who required a large labour force, they followed the example of Spain and Portugal and turned to Africa, and African slaves were brought to work on English plantations. Tobacco galvanised the demand for slave labour, followed by cotton, sugar cane, indigo and rice.

Laws in the South made things clear: slaves were forbidden to marry, own property, be educated or earn their freedom. In 1640, Maryland became the first colony to institutionalise slavery, and the following year Massachusetts stated that 'bondage was legal'. At that moment, slaves became property that could be bought and sold by their masters. A 1662 Virginia law confirmed that African captives were slaves for life. Rape of a female slave was not considered a crime unless it represented trespassing on another's property. Slaves were executed on suspicion of serious crimes by hanging or burning alive. Education was illegal and teachers, if caught, were punished and imprisoned for defying such laws. One African teacher, John Chavis, secretly operated a school in North Carolina for 30 years, without discovery from the authorities.

From 1680 to 1730, the Anglican Church in Virginia debated giving Christian teaching to slaves, but their efforts were blocked by slave owners, who feared that Africans would not remain enslaved if they converted to Christianity. They claimed that blacks were inferior to whites and deserved to be slaves.

With the advance of mechanisation, slave labour became less important globally, but the opposite proved true in America. The cotton gin was introduced after 1800 and prepared cotton for marketing so rapidly that the demand for slave labour increased rather than decreased.

Racism used to control the business

Greek society accepted Aristotle's notion that one race was born to serve another. People became property. Property could be sold.

Although slavery was practised throughout the world, slavery

SLAVERY NOW – AND THEN

was never considered an African institution or associated primarily with Africa, and Europeans were in captivity when the transatlantic slave trade started.

As the slave traders plundered the African continent, slavery and Africa became identical. Yet this brand of slavery is a modern invention. Before the sixteenth century there is almost no literary or artistic reference to suggest that Africans were considered inferior. When Michelangelo decided to immortalise slavery in marble, he chose a white man as a model. Before the transatlantic slave trade, there was no apparent racial prejudice where white people considered themselves superior to people of different races.

As the slave trade developed, a racist ideology emerged to justify the trade. Africans were said to be subhuman, uncivilised and inferior. As they were 'not one of us', they could be bought and sold. The slave trade could not have continued without this philosophy.

Charles Darwin developed a theory of evolution which placed Anglo-Saxons, that is, the British, at the top of the evolutionary scale, with Africans as a 'primitive' race. The British Empire grew from the conceit that 'the British were the best race to rule the world', as expressed by Cecil Rhodes, who founded the British colony of Rhodesia (now Zimbabwe) in Central Africa.

The biblical story of Noah and his sons was interpreted to justify slavery, with his disrespectful son, Ham, cursed to serve his brothers. As the slave trade developed, Ham was identified with African people, and therefore justified their enslavement.

Some plantation owners used Christianity to keep slaves in their 'place'. Poor and disadvantaged Christian slaves were required to be obedient in order to be rewarded in paradise. Preachers and missionaries were frequently accused of stirring up trouble by sharing the Christian message of freedom and equality amongst the slave population.

After slave trading became economically and socially acceptable in Europe, Africans were cast as inferior and despised.

How many slaves were sold?

The total population of Africa in 1500 was estimated at 47 million. Over the next 350 years, between 10 and 15 million Africans are thought to have been stolen from their country. Between four and six million are believed to have died during their capture or on the crossing. This excluded the millions of Africans abducted and sold as a result of the trans-Saharan slave trade. The statistics below are reproduced from Hugh Thomas's estimates in *The Slave Trade*. There are discrepancies in all the figures.

SLAVE NUMBERS
How many were sold?

Country	Voyages	Slaves transported
Portugal (including Brazil)	30,000	4,650,000
Spain (including Cuba)	4,000	1,600,000
France (including French West Indies)	4,200	1,250,000
Holland	2,000	500,000
Britain	12,000	2,600,000
British North America and US	1,500	300,000
Denmark	250	50,000
Other	250	50,000
Total	**54,200**	**11,000,000**

Where did they come from?

Senegambia (in Argiun), Sierra Leone	2,000,000
Windward Coast	250,000
Ivory Coast	250,000
Gold Coast (Ashanti)	1,500,000
Slave Coast (Dahomey, Adra, Oyo)	2,000,000
Benin to Calabar	2,000,000
Cameroons/Gabon	250,000
Loango	750,000

Congo/Angola	3,000,000
Mozambique/Madagascar	1,000,000
Total leaving African ports	**13,000,000**

Where did they go?

Brazil	4,000,000
Spanish empire (including Cuba)	2,500,000
British West Indies	2,000,000
French West Indies (including Cayenee)	1,600,000
British North America and US	500,000
Dutch West Indies (including Surinam)	500,000
Danish West Indies	28,000
Europe (including Portugal, Canary Islands, Madeira, Azores, etc.)	200,000
Total	**11,328,000**

How were they used?

Sugar plantations	5,000,000
Coffee plantations	2,000,000
Mines	1,000,000
Domestic labour	2,000,000
Cotton fields	500,000
Cocoa fields	250,000
Building	250,000
Total	**11,000,000**

THE BUSINESS OF SLAVERY

The campaign to end the slave trade

Turning point

It is said that the fabulous riches of the sugar boom of the late eighteenth century can be compared to the oil wealth of the Middle East. It was a period of great prosperity, with sugar the most important commodity in Europe. At the time, only a crank or an extremist would have suggested that the slave trade was wrong and should be stopped. Besides, everyone was involved – royalty, parliamentarians, churchmen, prominent personalities, the celebrities of the age.

Yet, in two decades, the greatest international human rights campaign ever seen had brought about the end of the slave trade, and within 50 years had contributed to the end of slavery.

The campaign had turned into a national movement united by a few simple ideas: that Christian England had built and established the institution of slavery – but that it was evil; that the system could be changed and individuals could play a part.

It started in Mincing Lane in 1765, when Granville Sharp, an affluent young civil servant, saw an African, aged about 16 or 17, collapsed in the street. The slave had been brought to England from the Caribbean, but his owner David Lisle, a lawyer from Barbados, had beaten him savagely and thrown the African youth into the street. Lisle hit the boy so hard on his head with a pistol that the weapon broke.

'I could hardly walk, or see my way, where I was going,' Jonathon Strong would recall later.

Sharp, a devout Christian and one of the founders of the British Bible Society, decided not to look the other way, but chose to get involved. He took Strong to St Bartholomew's Hospital, where he was treated for four and a half months, and then found him employment.

Two years later, Lisle recognised his former slave in the street and realised that he was, once again, a valuable property. He followed Strong home, and without repossessing his former slave, sold the youth to a Jamaican planter for £30. Lisle then hired two slave hunters, who kidnapped Strong and had him jailed until the next ship should sail for the West Indies.

Strong smuggled a letter out of his London prison cell to Granville Sharp, who demanded his release and later won his freedom, arguing that African slaves were entitled to protection on English soil. Strong's original owner was so enraged that he challenged Sharp to a duel. Strong never fully recovered from his beating and died in 1773.

Over the next few years, Sharp tested the legal system and tangled with the Chief Justice, Lord Mansfield, over cases of slaves in England. Sharp was determined to prove that slavery was illegal under the constitution and that no act of parliament authorised the keeping of slaves in England. It was just taken for granted by slave owners. But in each case that Sharp fought, the ownership of the slave was in dispute.

In 1771 he heard about James Somerset, a runaway slave who had been recaptured and was in chains on a ship bound for Jamaica, due to be sold again there. This time there was no doubt that the owner had the right to his slave. Sharp intervened, and the case came before Lord Mansfield again. England's Chief Justice urged the parties to settle out of court, and even asked parliament for new legislation.

Eventually, England's highest criminal court ruled that a slave owner had no right to deport his slave from English soil. Lord Mansfield concluded, '*Fiat justitia ruat coelum*' ('Let justice be done though the skies fall').

James Somerset was set free, but Lord Mansfield's ruling ended at England's shore. Across the sea, nothing had changed.

Lord Mansfield had not declared slavery illegal, but it was a turning point in the history of slavery and a triumph for Sharp, Britain's first anti-slavery campaigner. It had taken Sharp seven years and a string of legal cases to demonstrate that no man could hold property rights over another in England.

Mansfield's court ruling was widely misinterpreted. Mike Kaye has noted that the Chief Justice of England was hesitant to decide if the right to property was more important than the right to freedom, and he was careful not to set a precedent. Yet both sides of the dispute thought that he had made slavery illegal in England. It became important what people thought he had said, rather than the exact text, and the press and public opinion understood that slaves were freed once they reached England. This was not in the ruling, but the myth spread. Despite this, slave owners acted as though nothing had changed – they continued to advertise auctions and sales, and runaways were hunted down.

Word spread that Granville Sharp was a friend of slaves in Britain, and one of the people who knocked on his door was Olaudah Equiano.

After his capture, Equiano had been taken to the English colony of Barbados in the West Indies, but no one purchased the child. He was then sold to a plantation in Virginia, and sold on again to a British naval officer, who changed his name. He learned to read and write and was eventually able to purchase his freedom. Equiano became a Christian and was baptised at St Margaret's, Westminster, the official parish church of the House of Commons.

Equiano had tried to rescue a friend who had been kidnapped in London and put on a ship sailing for the West Indies. With brilliant skill, he whitened his face and served the slave owner with a court summons, but this time there was no happy ending. Equiano turned to Sharp for help, but they were unable to obtain the slave's return or to prevent his early tortured death in slavery.

In March 1783, Equiano called again on Granville Sharp and told him about the notorious affair of the *Zong*, a Liverpool slave ship that had sailed from Africa to Jamaica with 440 slaves on board. After many had died through illness, the *Zong*'s captain, Luke Collingwood, threw 132 sick slaves overboard, knowing he could collect insurance money for slaves 'lost at sea', but not for those who died from illness. When the ship's owners claimed the insurance money, the firm would not pay out and the case went to court in London's Guildhall.

After hearing Equiano's story, Sharp decided to bring a murder charge against the ship's captain. One day when he was in court, the *Zong*'s lawyers, infuriated by his threat, looked directly at Sharp and, referring to the murder charge, said, 'It would be madness: the blacks were property.'

Again, Lord Mansfield dragged out the case, commenting that murder was irrelevant. It was 'just as if horses were killed'.

The *Zong*'s owners won £3,960 compensation, but a second trial proved that the ship's captain had lied when citing a lack of water on board as the reason for the massacre. Sharp failed to get anyone prosecuted, and the case never made headline news, although 50 years later it became the subject for one of Turner's most celebrated paintings, *Slave Ship*.

At the time, Sharp and Equiano were probably the only two who had taken direct action to help slaves in England.

But things were changing.

Two years after the *Zong* incident, Cambridge University offered a prize for a literary competition on slavery, and a young divinity student decided to enter. The student knew little about the topic, but his research stirred him deeply, and his passionate essay won him the contest. Sometime later, he experienced 'a direct revelation from God ordering him to devote his life to abolishing the trade'.

The student's name was Thomas Clarkson. The campaign to end the slave trade had found one of its central commanders.

The leaders of the campaign

In London, Clarkson met people who were equally dedicated to the cause that had captured his heart.

At the centre of things were the Quakers, who had already formed a committee and petitioned parliament in 1783 against the slave trade.

The Quakers had taken action in America 40 years earlier. In 1743, a young Quaker named John Woolman had been asked by his employer to write out a bill of sale for a slave. Woolman obeyed, but the incident never left his mind. He realised that his own hand had sentenced another man into bondage. When asked to do this again, he refused, and declared that slave keeping was 'a practice inconsistent with the Christian religion'.

Woolman vowed never to be used in the system of slavery again. He replaced sugar with maple syrup, refused to wear dyed clothes, because slaves worked on dyes, and pressed the Quaker communities to free their slaves. As a result, Quakers were the first group to denounce slavery. They had been fined vast sums of money in Barbados during the seventeenth century for encouraging slaves to become Christians, and for accepting them into their church. Quakers at that time were concerned over the conditions in which slaves were held, but had not called for an end to slavery.

On the 22nd May 1787, nine Quakers and, among others, Granville Sharp and Thomas Clarkson, formed a pressure group called the Society for the Abolition of the Slave Trade. The name of the group was significant. While some wanted an end to slavery itself, it was not to be their primary objective. Their logic was simple: with an end to the trade in slaves, slavery would die out.

The immediate task was to establish the facts, and Clarkson threw himself into the research assignment with the dedication of a Pulitzer Prize-winning investigative journalist. The entire campaign relied on his discoveries, and he did not disappoint.

Second, the group needed a parliamentary leader. They turned to a wealthy young MP from Hull, William Wilberforce.

One year earlier, Wilberforce had made a decision to become an evangelical Christian and, like Clarkson, was wondering what he should do with his life. While Clarkson abandoned a career in the church and decided that God wanted to use him to address the contemporary evil of slavery, Wilberforce was looking the other way, wondering if his future lay in the church, rather than politics. Wilberforce sometimes slipped a pebble into his shoe to keep himself focused on spiritual things.

Wilberforce talked with his friend, Prime Minister William Pitt, before accepting the anti-slave-trade assignment. The prime minister shared his faith and was against the slave trade, and Wilberforce took on the challenge to lead the campaign in parliament.

In time, other figures would emerge, but the driving force of the Quakers, Sharp, Clarkson and Wilberforce, supported by key Africans such as Equiano, and their shared common faith, both compelled and motivated them to fight the great evil of their age. Without these hands at the wheel, the process would have taken longer and could have strayed wide off the mark. Although there were disagreements (some wanted the campaign to end slavery and not just the slave trade) and tensions (Wilberforce did not want women to collect petitions or to take an active part in the campaign), their commitment remained resolute and contributed to extraordinary action: the end of the slave trade and, eventually, slavery as a whole.

The first human rights campaign

Today we accept and expect particular instruments in any campaign, but many of the devices outlined below were first used by the committee of the Society for the Abolition of the Slave Trade. Kevin Bales and Adam Hochshchild both outlined how this resulted in a national movement that changed public opinion.

Research

Clarkson travelled thousands of miles, interviewed countless seamen, visited hundreds of ships, tabulated copious statistics and compiled numerous reports. He boarded slave ships and measured them, revealing that vessels were carrying higher numbers of slaves than they had been built to hold. He collected shackles, thumbscrews, mouth-openers and other tools of torture that were used on slave ships, but produced in England, and he displayed them to stunned audiences. Clarkson's reports roused parliament and the country. Without this factual documentation, the campaign would never have made the impact it did.

Clarkson's research also exposed the shocking effect the slave trade was having on English sailors, with a high percentage dying on these horrifying journeys.

Newsletters and leaflets

Black Cargoes calculated that 26,526 reports and 51,432 books and pamphlets were circulated in the first 15 months of the campaign.

Fundraising

Granville Sharp personally signed letters that were hand-delivered to donors. It has been called history's first direct-mail fundraising letter. Initially, about 2,000 people contributed funds, and they had contacts in 39 countries.

Publicity and marketing

Josiah Wedgwood, designated Potter to the Queen, had a flair for promotion and designed the defining image of the campaign: a kneeling African with the phrase 'Am I not a man and a brother'. Perceived by some today as degrading, this image was an instant hit, with merchandise reproduced widely. It became a popular fashion accessory for young ladies.

Logo

Wedgwood's image was seen everywhere and became identified as the brand of the abolition campaign. This was probably the first time a logo had been used in this way for such a campaign.

Posters

The most graphic image of the time was a drawing produced by Clarkson that showed how slaves were packed on board a slave ship, the *Brookes*. The image had a huge impact and was widely reproduced on fliers, leaflets and posters.

Press

Equiano, among others, used the press regularly and wrote letters and articles for London newspapers.

Public meetings

Clarkson travelled thousands of miles on horseback to speak at packed meetings, mostly in churches, all over the country. Equiano also travelled widely, including across Scotland and Ireland, to talk about his experiences as a slave in Africa.

Awareness

Clarkson and Wilberforce led the campaign, but Africans like Equiano made a huge contribution, providing the authentic voice that gave strength, character and uniqueness to the cause. Another freed slave in London, Ottobah Cugoana, produced publications that raised the stakes. He used scriptures to challenge his readers to go beyond the abolition of the slave trade and to address the evil of slavery itself, and proposed the 'universal emancipation of slaves', something the abolition committee had not done.

Lobbying

Equiano regularly lobbied MPs, and led a black delegation to the House of Commons to meet the prime minister. Decades later, campaigners, especially women, lobbied MPs to vote for anti-slavery legislation.

Petitions

The first national petition was launched in 1788, and in 1792 the largest number of petitions ever submitted on a single issue was handed in to parliament. Women played an influential role in ensuring its success.

Boycott

When parliament rejected one of Wilberforce's bills in 1791, the campaign proposed a practical response: about 300,000 people refused to use West Indian sugar and substituted honey or maple syrup instead. One church leader carried syrup with him, so that if his parishioners offered him a cup of tea, he would be ready. At the time sugar was England's largest import, and the opposition's publicity insisted that consumers were running a risk to their constitution by dropping sugar from their diet. One eager physician even recommended that it should be used for cleaning teeth.

Publications

Equiano published his life story and it became one of the most significant documents in the campaign. His *Interesting Narrative* was a smash hit, reprinted frequently, translated widely and, at that point, the only book from England to be published in the US. He pre-sold copies, thus raising capital for the book's production, offering discounts for bulk orders. The book had a wide circulation amongst royalty, parliament and church leaders. He organised a lengthy book tour, held public meetings and inspired people to join the campaign.

Equiano's sheer presence in England was an unimaginable boost, and successfully combated public opinion, which classified Africans as wild, heathen savages. Here was an articulate, intelligent African man who was a Christian and had earned his freedom.

Popular artists, poets and writers also covered the topic of slavery, including William Blake's illustrations on slave torture, Wordsworth's sonnet to the rebel leader Toussaint L'Ouverture, Jane Austen's *Mansfield Park*, Thackeray's *Vanity Fair*, Daniel Defoe's *Robinson Crusoe*, and the works of the Brontës. Poet William Cowper's sarcasm was clear:

> I own I am shocked at the purchase of slaves
> And fear those who buy them and sell them are knaves
> What I hear of their hardships, their tortures and groans
> Is almost enough to draw pity from stones
>
> I pity them greatly, but I must be mum
> For how could we do without sugar and rum?
> Especially sugar, so needful we see
> What? Give up our desserts, our coffee and tea!

Political action

Wilberforce became a focal point for parliamentary action. He exerted pressure on parliament through the use of petitions and was supported by several strategic figures such as James Stephen. Women played an important role, and during parliamentary elections in 1826, Elizabeth Heyrick urged people only to vote for MPs who would support the campaign.

Despite all the reports, statistics, speeches and publicity, the presence of Africans, both freed and former slaves, such as Equiano in England gave the campaign its character and power as they spoke out against the atrocities they had experienced.

Ottobah Cugoana was born in present-day Ghana, enslaved as a teenager and brought to England from Grenada. He secured his freedom in 1788 and was a servant to Richard Cosway, the court painter. He was the first African to demand the end of slavery. His tract *On the Evil of Slavery*, written in 1787, argued:

> . . . kings are the ministers of God, to do justice, and not to bear the sword in vain, but revenge wrath upon them that do evil. But if they do not in such a case as this, the cruel oppressions of thousands, and the blood of the murdered Africans who slain by the sword of cruel avarice, must rest upon their own guilty heads . . .

Cugoana apparently clashed with Wilberforce over the latter's distinction between the slave trade and the end of slavery. In 1807, the influential parliamentarian wrote, 'It would be wrong to emancipate [the slaves]. To grant freedom to them immediately, would be to insure not only their master's ruin, but their own. They must [first] be trained and educated for freedom.'

Ignatius Sancho had been born on a slave ship and came to England, aged two, in 1731. He was owned by three sisters who did not believe that enslaved Africans should be educated, but he was self-taught and became the first African prose writer to have his work published in England. He wrote poetry, plays and songs and composed music for violin, mandolin, flute and harpsichord. Gainsborough painted his portrait and he was embraced by London's artistic community.

The History of Mary Prince, a gripping story, was the first book by a female African slave to be published in Britain. It created a sensation in 1831 and was reprinted three times that same year. Mary was born in Bermuda, the daughter of slaves, who escaped after her 'master' brought her to England in 1828, and wrote of the cruelty she had endured: 'To strip me naked – to hang me up by the wrists and lay my flesh open with cow-skin, was an ordinary punishment for even a slight offence.'

Slaves branded with church logo

Royalty, parliamentarians and the elite of the day found it acceptable to own slaves. So did the church.

The Church of England's Society for the Propagation of the Gospel (SPG) became slave owners in 1740, when they inherited the Codrington plantation, the second largest in Barbados. Every slave had the word 'society' branded on their chest to remind them of their owners in England, as the SPG had given over the operational responsibilities to local planters.

Thirty years after the church took it over, four out of every ten slaves died within three years. Some have suggested that this was a deliberate 'work to death' policy, as the slave owners relied on a steady supply of slaves from Africa and the remote church owners were primarily concerned with profit. Profits funded churches in England and established Oxford's All Souls College, according to James Walvin.

The Church of England was not alone. Hugh Thomas claimed that George Fox, the founder of the Quakers, owned slaves in Pennsylvania, along with William Penn, the founder of the colony, and the renowned preacher George Whitefield.

The established churches found it difficult to extricate themselves. As the message from new evangelical churches took hold, they became champions of the cause. With England in the grip of a revival, and with churches packed, the message of anti-slavery and Christian responsibility thundered from pulpits across the land. It was the churches that promoted the petitions against the slave trade and shaped the emerging grass-roots protest movement.

The true Christian message of redemption and justice, led by John Wesley and others, countered the racist thinking from people such as Sir Rose Price, a baronet, who argued that slavery 'was God's will for black men, and that they were treated kindly by their white owners'.

The campaign hits the road

The committee that came together to fight the slave trade invented the prototype of modern protest and it has been called the world's first human rights campaign.

The campaign had two phases. First, the end of the slave trade, from 1787 to 1807; and second, the attack on slavery itself, from 1823 to 1838.

The political system needed a navigator of exceptional skill, and Wilberforce proved he was the man for the job. He used Clarkson's research to maximum effect, and in 1788 the movement seemed unstoppable.

In that same year, John Newton spoke for the first time about his experience as a slave ship captain. Newton had been enslaved himself, and once, near death on the Guinea coast, had survived when slaves waiting to be sold shared their meagre rations with him. After ten years at sea, Newton turned his back on the trade and became a Christian minister, well known for writing hymns such as 'Amazing Grace' and 'How Sweet the Name of Jesus Sounds'. Yet, in 30 years of ministry, he had never spoken about the slave trade and still retained links with the business. However, when he did speak in 1788, his words were of significance because he was an important figure in London circles with an influential parish in the city.

That same year, Sir William Dolben led a group of MPs onto a slave ship docked in the Thames. He introduced a parliamentary bill to limit the number of slaves a ship could carry, and it was quickly adopted.

Under pressure, parliament set up hearings, from 1790 to 1791, to investigate the slave trade, and in conclusion Wilberforce tabled a motion for a ban on trading slaves. This was defeated by 163 votes to 88. In Liverpool, church bells rang out to mark and celebrate the occasion. The following year, 1792, he tried again, and a watered-down version was passed, recommending a gradual end to the slave trade. This died in the House of Lords, as did another bill, the following year.

Five years passed. The committee had been active. Sharp had been busy with a colony for freed slaves in Sierra Leone. Adam Smith, often called the first economist, had published an influential study suggesting that slave labour was not profitable, and the idea was gaining ground. Meanwhile, the pro-slavery lobby was promoting the benefits of slavery and the danger of its abolition. Captain Tobin told the House of Commons that conditions on his ship were like 'a nursery in any private family', with the crew 'making everything as comfortable as possible for the slaves'. Lord Nelson spoke of the 'damnable doctrine of Wilberforce and his hypocritical allies'. The campaign had made its mark, but in reality only one law had been passed, and hopes of any political breakthrough were dashed by overseas events.

In St-Dominque (modern Haiti) the largest slave revolt ever seen spread panic among slave owners. In 1793, the war with France brought the anti-slavery campaign to a standstill.

THE COLONY IN SIERRA LEONE

During the American War of Independence, England offered slaves of rebel Americans their freedom if they revolted. The English tactic worked and slaves fled their master's southern plantations to cross into British lines. The slaves were taken to Nova Scotia, but the initiative broke down. A slave, Thomas Peters, was determined to fight for their rights, and travelled to London, gaining the support of the black community, then the abolitionists, and finally the government. It was through Peters that Granville Sharp got involved, and Thomas Clarkson's brother, John, took an active part in getting a group to Sierra Leone. In Rough Crossing, Simon Schama concludes, 'The story in the end turned to one of tragedy, where the idea of a free black country became subsumed by British promises that were continually hedged and qualified. In 1808, Sierra Leone became just another imperial colony.'

THE CAMPAIGN TO END THE SLAVE TRADE

The revolt in St-Dominque (modern Haiti)

St-Dominque had a slave labour force of 465,000, the largest in the Caribbean, and its 8,000 plantations accounted for over one third of France's foreign trade, according to Adam Hochschild. It produced over half the world's coffee and in 1787 exported almost as much sugar as Jamaica, Cuba and Brazil combined. Conditions for slaves had been described as the 'worst hell on earth' and revolts had flared up, leading to a revolution in August 1791 that became a turning point in its history. The rebellion was the largest and the worst ever seen, with deaths, rapes and horrific mutilations. The slaves held off forces from France, Britain and Spain, under their commander, General Toussaint L'Ouverture. Although he was captured, the resistance endured, and on the 1st January 1804, Haiti was declared the first black independent state, and the first to end plantation slavery. Of all the revolts, this was the only one that succeeded in overthrowing the slave system.

The revolt demonstrated what was possible. To the slave world, it was clear that freedom was attainable; the slave owners feared a similar fate, and that abolition would lead to economic disaster and slaughter for Europeans.

The age of revolution, with its emphasis on rights and equality, had spread ideas of liberation, starting with American independence in 1776 and the French Revolution in 1789. But were these rights available to Africans?

How the slave trade ended

Slave resistance

African slaves in captivity did not accept their position of servitude with passivity and resignation, and neither did they receive their freedom as victims. In every circumstance available to them, they clutched at anything that would bring freedom.

Just running away was a personal step of resistance, despite the torture they knew they would face if they were captured.

Runaways were known as 'maroons', from a Spanish word meaning stray cattle that return to the wild. Throughout the history of slavery, running away was a persistent form of rebellion.

In *The Atlas of Slavery*, James Walvin recorded 493 known revolts on slave ships and 65 revolts in North America, among other plots. In 1546, over 7,000 maroons were living in Santo Domingo's heavily wooded mountains.

In Brazil, the maroon community of Palmares in Alagoas survived throughout most of the seventeenth century. When their leader, Zumbi, was captured and beheaded in 1695, his followers committed mass suicide, rather than be re-enslaved.

The steps leading up to the 1807 slave bill

Britain obtained Dutch and French territories in the West Indies, including Trinidad and Guyana, but plantation owners in the Caribbean saw this as alarming competition, since the new lands were fertile and ripe for sugar cultivation. As a tactic they suggested ending the slave trade for a few years: this would have stopped their rivals from importing the labour force needed to cultivate the sugar crop.

In England, James Stephen shared Wilberforce's faith and supported his parliamentary campaign, but grew frustrated with the slow progress. Stephen spotted a strategic opportunity and suggested a different approach, with a new bill aimed at limiting English trade with colonies of France and its allies.

It was a brilliant tactic. Who could argue with a strategy that restricted trade with England's old enemy? David Davies noted in *Inhuman Bondage*, 'Napoleon's restoration of slavery and the slave trade suddenly made abolition compatible with patriotic hostility to the French.'

The debate was brief, slavery was barely mentioned, even Wilberforce did not speak, and the bill sailed through the Commons. By the time it passed the Lords, however, everyone had woken up to the implications, and when it returned to the Commons, things became tense. This was the first time in a decade that the issue had been debated with such seriousness in both houses of parliament. With intensive lobbying from each side, a historic victory was in the making. Early in 1807, 20 years after the campaign had been launched, parliament finally approved a bill that abolished the British slave trade. From the 1st January 1808, it became illegal for any English ship to carry slaves.

This did not end the slave trade. It made no difference to Africans in slavery around the world, and it was still legal to own slaves. English ships carried on slaving, sailing under different flags, and dodged the English navy boats that had been commissioned to enforce the new law.

That same year, the US also tried to ban the slave trade, but the demand for slaves in the cotton-growing states was so intensive that smuggling became common.

Nonetheless, the 1807 bill was a significant victory for everyone involved in campaigning, and a tremendous boost for all those who had faithfully supported the committee's work.

A new campaign to end slavery, 1823–38

Fifteen years after the 1807 bill, a few things were clear: banning the trade had not resulted in the end of slavery, and the conditions for slaves had not improved in the plantations. Instead, the slave trade was booming.

Wilberforce was to pass the parliamentary mantle to Thomas Buxton, a fellow evangelical, and a new group formed: the London Society for Mitigating and Gradually Abolishing the State of Slavery. The name reflected the hesitancy. Feeling little pressure, parliament passed resolutions encouraging religious instruction for slaves, and stopped the whipping of slave women.

Women around the country were discovering their voice, none more influential than the Quaker Elizabeth Heyrick. She was to become the dynamo of the movement, unafraid to challenge the order of the day. She was not going to accept a 'gradual' abolition of slavery. She wanted an end. She wanted it immediately. She confronted the established abolition group directly and published a leaflet which said it all: 'Immediate not gradual abolition'. Heyrick was sympathetic to the revolts in the West Indies, and wrote, 'Was it not in the cause of self-defence from the most degrading, intolerable oppression?' She asked why their revolts were any less 'heroic and meritorious' than the Greek battle for independence from the Turks. Pushing the boundaries of the day, she encouraged women to get involved, and over 70 women's groups emerged. She publicised a new sugar boycott and travelled around Leicester, visiting every city grocer, asking them not to stock sugar grown by slaves. When parliamentary elections were held in 1826, she urged people only to vote for candidates who supported immediate abolition.

The women's committees threatened to withhold their annual donation of £50 to the central abolition group unless they dropped 'gradual' from their title. In 1833, parliament received petitions signed by nearly 1.5 million people, of whom 350,000 were women.

Amidst this activity, the slaves themselves played an important part. As the number and scale of the revolts increased, the fear spread amongst Europeans and forced the authorities to act. The major rebellions were as follows.

1816, Barbados

An uprising led by a slave called Bussa was crushed. Four hundred slaves were executed, others were flogged and sent to Sierra Leone.

1823, Demerara (Guyana)

This was known as one of the worst frontiers for brutalising slaves. Ironically, large numbers had become Christians and attended church. Twelve thousand slaves were involved in the rebellion, demanding freedom as well as the right to worship on Sundays. The revolt was brutally stamped out, with 250 slaves killed in mass shootings, formal executions and dismembered victims on public display. Christian leaders were accused of incitement and John Smith, a London Missionary Society worker trusted by the slaves, was arrested and imprisoned, but died accidentally in his prison cell. In England, Smith's death had a huge impact.

1831, America

A rebellion led by Nat Turner, a slave and religious mystic who could read and write, terrified the American South. It took several thousand troops to crush the uprising.

1831–2, Jamaica

This revolt (the 'Baptist Wars') of Christian slaves was led by Sam Sharpe from Montego Bay, who had a formidable reputation as a slave preacher. The authorities refused to allow slaves to celebrate Christmas Day in 1831, even though it fell on a Sunday, and in retaliation over 20,000 slaves were involved in the greatest slave uprising ever seen in the British Caribbean. Methodist missionaries later paid tribute to Sharpe's authority by revealing that several freemen had supported the struggle for freedom, and a white plantation official had even shown the rebels how to make bullets.

The revolt caused huge damage to plantations, and 14 whites were killed in the battle to regain control. The rebels held out for almost a month, but they were defeated and over 500 slaves were killed.

The planters accused the Christians of stirring up trouble, and a local newspaper called for the missionaries to be hanged. About 20 Baptist and Methodist chapels were burned to the ground. Missionaries were jailed; one was beaten and tarred, but was saved from being set on fire by black supporters, who arrived just in time. Sharpe was sentenced to death, but while in jail he told one missionary, 'I would rather die on those gallows than live in slavery.'

After Sharpe was hanged, his owners were paid £16.10s compensation for their loss of property.

Reverend Hope Waddell, a Presbyterian missionary, noted that despite the torment of 'these sugar estates, the causes and scenes of their [the slaves'] life-long trials and degradation, tears and blood', their restraint was compelling: 'Amid the wild excitement of the night, not one freeman's life was taken, not one freewoman molested by the insurgent slaves.'

When the missionaries returned to England, churches were shocked to hear their first-hand reports about how Christian slaves and missionaries were treated, and churches burned. One missionary's report, 'Three Months in Jamaica', sold 20,000 copies in two weeks.

One week after the hanging of Sam Sharpe, parliament set up a committee to investigate how slavery could be ended.

The end of slavery

The evidence was in and the outcome inevitable. These were the final days of slavery. The debate in parliament lasted over three months. The sticking point was this: what compensation should be paid to the slave owners for the loss of their property rights?

The question provoked outrage and protests. Churches and abolitionists argued that slavery was illegal, therefore there could be no compensation.

Parliament first proposed a loan of £15 million as compensation, but in time this became a gift of £20 million paid to all slave owners – for the loss of their property. The sum of £20 million equalled 40 per cent of the national budget of the day (calculated to be about $3.3 billion in 2005).

In 1833, an act of parliament was finally passed ending slavery, and £20 million compensation was paid to all slave owners. The Church of England collected £8,823 (about $950,000 in 2005) for its 411 slaves on the Codrington plantation. The bishop of Exeter and three business colleagues were paid nearly £13,000 to compensate them for the loss of 665 slaves in 1833.

As many plantations were mortgaged, Adam Hochschild reported, it was London creditors who pocketed the money.

Parliament also decided that slavery would end in two parts: slaves would have to work as 'apprentices' for their owners for twelve years before they could be freed. After pressure, the apprentice or unpaid slave-like labour scheme was reduced from twelve to six years, and eventually to four years.

The true end of slavery came five years later, on the 1st August 1838, when nearly one million African men, women and children throughout the British Empire were no longer enslaved and became officially free.

Former slaves celebrated the moment in churches and chapels. James Walvin, in *History Magazine*, wrote, 'Contrary to the fears of whites in the islands, slavery, born in, and sustained by violence, ended peacefully and at prayer.'

In Jamaica, a midnight thanksgiving service was held in one chapel with a coffin inscribed 'Colonial Slavery died July 31st, 1838, aged 276 years'.

A FAIR SHARE?
The slave owners got £20 million for their property. The slaves got nothing. Slaves had to work an additional four years. Freedom had come.

Why slavery ended

So why did the greatest superpower of the age finally end slavery?

The slave revolts played a critical part, alongside the sugar protests and campaigning in England. But there were other reasons.

At the time only a minority of the population could vote, and only candidates with an income of £300 per annum, £600 in places, were allowed to stand as MPs. But parliament had undergone a transformation with massive reforms, and by 1832 the process had been completed, opening the vote to all but the poorest men. Old pro-slavery MPs had been swept from power, replaced by many who favoured abolition. Moreover, the campaign pressured MPs to support the anti-slavery bills, or they would be voted out at future elections. When the new towns and cities, like Manchester, were given a voice for the first time, they used it for issues that had concerned them in the past, and slavery was one of these.

The profits of slavery became less enticing. Wealthy investors found that profits were lucrative and more reliable with local businesses, rather than with ships and slaves. In an essay for *Transatlantic Slavery*, James Walvin explained, 'It was not so much that slavery became unprofitable, rather that other forms of economic activity were more attractive, less risky and more controlled.'

By the mid-1820s, England's population lived in an urbanised environment, and with emerging industrialisation came a rising spirit that viewed slavery differently. In a world where ideas of liberty and freedom were being explored and advanced, slavery seemed offensive. With literacy growing, it was easier for printed literature to circulate and ideas to form. For the first time, popular literature gripped interest and culture. Women were playing an important role, and Elizabeth Heyrick was one such pioneer.

Equally significant was the spirit in the nation that had emerged from the influence of the Christian message.

Most of the petitions that had stormed parliament had been collected in churches, and this grass-roots support had maintained the campaign and given it structure and focus. When missionaries returned from overseas, people learned the truth of plantation life directly from those who had experienced it first-hand. Christians in England were horrified to hear how fellow believers such as John Smith had been treated, that churches had been burnt, and that slave owners tortured Christian slaves. This intensified their zeal to end the institution of slavery.

In this context, the Christian leadership of the anti-slavery campaign group used the economic and social changes in England, and became the catalyst for change for the slaves of Africa.

James Walvin, in *History Magazine*, emphasised the impact that the Christian faith had on slaves. 'It is hard to underestimate the importance of black Christianity. It provided a place to worship away from the plantation, where slaves could gather on their day of rest. It provided a language and vivid imagery, from the Bibles and hymns, which spoke directly to the slave experience.'

In time, powerful slave preachers emerged who drew inspiration from historical incidents of people in bondage waiting for freedom and salvation. The slave protesters were seeking freedom and the right to worship. And freedom, when it came in 1838, was celebrated in churches.

After slavery

Slavery did not end in a blaze of violence as predicted, but in services of thanksgiving. It was white 'civilised' slave owners who had acted offensively, protecting their business empires, while slaves such as Sam Sharpe had demonstrated true dignity, character and faith.

S. I. Martin and Hugh Thomas both reported that the only

British national on trial for trading slaves was Pedro Zuleta, a naturalised Briton of Spanish origin and a commercial agent and banker to Pedro Blanco, the leading slave trader in West Africa in the 1840s. After one and a half hours' deliberation, the jury found him not guilty.

Mike Morris, in a paper for Peaceworks, observed that while families were destroyed in Africa, dynasties were birthed in England. Fortunes were made from the business of slavery, and today we walk by the evidence daily.

Sir Hans Sloane (yes, that Sloane Square in London) dealt in the sugar business and his wife had vast slave-based interests in Jamaica. His collections 'became the nucleus of the British Museum'. John Julius Angerstein oversaw the expansion of Lloyds of London as a major insurer of slave ships. He was an art enthusiast and his collection formed the core of the National Gallery. Other landmarks with slavery in their history include Oxford's All Souls College, London's Tate Gallery, the baroque palace in Middlesex built by the first Duke of Chandos, Harewood House, the former home of Queen Mary.

The labour shortages on the plantations were solved by a new form of bondage: indentured labour, or 'coolies', a word traced back to the Hindi *kuli*, or *quli*, meaning 'hired labourer'. Research by Prabhu P. Mohapatra suggested that 85 per cent of these 'coolies' were Hindus, and 32 per cent were Dalits or untouchables.

The predominantly Indian 'coolie' workforce was used in British colonies in the Caribbean, Indian Ocean, Africa and the Pacific. Mike Kaye, from Anti-Slavery International, reported that many had been deceived or coerced into signing contracts, and Mahatma Gandhi campaigned for their rights in South Africa in 1860. James Walvin, in *The Atlas of Slavery*, wrote, 'The result was an extraordinary migration of labouring people from their Indian homelands. By the time indentured labour was ended after the First World War, almost 1.5 million Indians had been shipped from India by the colonial power that trumpeted its virtue in abolishing slavery.'

The world's greatest slaving city of Liverpool adapted and continued to prosper, with many of the same slave merchants switching to palm oil, which became the main trading import for the next 100 years. Palm oil was extracted from the berries of palm trees and was in great demand in modern Britain. It was needed for new metal machinery, the textile industry and the railways; it was also needed for soap production, a demand that had increased as industrial workers took on dirtier jobs. The city also imported raw cotton produced by slave labour on plantations in America, and as late as 1860 an American slave ship allegedly picked up supplies in Liverpool. Streets named after slave merchants have survived and these include Earle, Cunliffe, Gildart, Tarleton and Bold. Penny Lane, made famous by the Beatles, was named after James Penny, a wealthy slave ship owner, but Liverpool officials decided to modify a proposal to rename streets linked to the slave trade.

The passing of time has given greater roles to some, neglecting others. Wilberforce's important position was boosted by a five-volume biography by his sons, both influential churchmen, but in these volumes Clarkson's role in the campaign was severely limited. In Clarkson's own book, he excluded the small though significant role played by James Stephen. Britain's carefully crafted image as the heroic champion that ended the slave trade obscured the huge part it played in slavery, and the huge profit it gained from it, which some have called the greatest act of historical amnesia.

Enforcement

Although Norway had been the first to ban slavery, it was England who demanded that all of Europe's slave-owning nations should follow their example, and the Royal Navy patrolled the 2,000-mile coastline of Africa enforcing the order.

1815	Sweden, Denmark and the Netherlands
1830	France
1850	Brazil
1867	Spain

THE END OF SLAVERY AND THE FREEING OF SLAVES

1847	Sweden
1848	Denmark, France
1863	Netherlands
1870–73	Spain
1886	Cuba

Revolutionary France abolished slavery in 1794, but reintroduced it in 1802, finally freeing its slaves in 1848.

THE CASE AGAINST SLAVERY

Moral: it was evil and un-Christian.

Economic: it was expensive and inefficient.

Legal: slavery was illegal under British law.

Problems in the plantations: slaves' resistance caused difficulties; education and Christianity encouraged a desire for freedom.

The North American slave experience

North America inherited the institution of slavery from the English at independence in 1776, but by the Civil War, 85 years later, slavery had developed into a distinctive structure.

When the Declaration of Independence was signed, slavery was legal in all 13 colonies. The slogan 'All men are created equal' proved paradoxical when the champions of liberty were themselves slave owners, including George Washington, Thomas Jefferson and Benjamin Franklin. It was a tragic contradiction at the heart of the American Revolution. Franklin owned slaves for 30 years and sold them at his general store. Later his ideas changed, and he started the first African school and argued for their freedom.

In a landmark case in 1856, Dred Scott was forbidden to seek his freedom in court because 'he was a Negro not just slave'. Chief Justice Roger B. Taney declared, 'No Negro whether slave or free could ever be considered a citizen of the United States within the meaning of the Constitution.'

Refugees from slavery fled from the South across the Ohio River to the North via the 'Underground Railroad', an invisible network of pathways, safe houses and signals, run mainly by Africans who helped runaway slaves to make their way to safety. From 1805 to 1895, about 100,000 Africans escaped.

Harriet Tubman was born a slave in Maryland in 1823, but escaped when she was 25 years old. Later, Harriet rescued her parents in the first of 19 secret trips she made to the South, when she guided over 300 slaves to freedom.

Slavery was not an issue in the North, where cold weather and poor soil made farming difficult, unlike in the South. Instead, the North concentrated on manufacturing and trade. The North wanted tariffs on imported foreign products to protect their new industries, but the South was still mainly agricultural and they relied on goods from abroad, so were against tariffs.

Tension over trade, politics, economics, industrialisation – and slavery – were among the main issues which divided the country, and Abraham Lincoln had been in office for one month when war broke out on the 12th April 1861. The Civil War involved 3 million people and 600,000 died in the conflict that lasted four years. It was the greatest war in American history and was the only war fought on American soil by Americans. After the war, African Americans were given some freedoms, but these were overturned and violent oppression followed, with groups such as the Ku Klux Klan spreading terror with kidnapping and lynching.

The struggle for civil rights took a dramatic turn in Montgomery,

Alabama in 1955, when Rosa Parks, a 42-year-old black American, refused to give up her seat to a white passenger, thereby breaking the law. The price for disobedience was jail, and Mrs Parks was arrested and fined $14. Rosa Parks was not the first to be arrested, but she was the first to challenge the system, and her action marked the start of the modern civil rights movement in America. Her arrest led to the desegregation of the transport system, after a 381-day boycott organised by a 26-year-old Baptist minister. It was in the heat of this protest that the organiser, Reverend Martin Luther King Jr, would discover a new calling on his life. The movement for justice was unstoppable and led to the 1964 Civil Rights Act, which made racial discrimination illegal in the US.

Rhythm and blues

There was no single 'African culture' that was exported, as slaves came from different parts of Africa with varied languages, traditions and influences. This was evident in their vibrant music, songs and dances that influenced – and, as with jazz, sometimes overtook – more traditional forms.

Slaves from Africa found temporary solace from their oppression in the music they had carried with them from their homelands, and their songs expressed both hope and despair.

Slave owners in Brazil allowed their slaves to continue their heritage by playing drums, while American slave owners feared that the drum beats were used as signals for communication, and outlawed them.

Brazilian sambas are rooted in the musical traditions of Angola, where many of the slaves had come from, and today Brazil's musical character is defined by its hypnotic rhythms and legendary samba dance music.

In America, deprived of drums, Africans timed their labour to the tempo of their music, and picking cotton and working on the railway became important themes in their songs.

As slaves entered American culture, the church became a regular part of their Sundays, and spirituals such as 'He's Got the Whole World in His Hands' brought comfort, as 'Go Down Moses' likened their oppression to that of the enslaved Israelites.

The crime of helping slaves to escape, or even inciting them to escape, was punishable by death. For this reason, slave songs had secret coded messages in their lyrics. Songs such as 'Wade in the Water' and 'Follow the Drinking Gourd' (parodied in the film *Life of Brian*) provided literal escape instructions and coded maps with details of escape. The titles were advice to runaways on how to avoid being tracked by bloodhounds. 'Steal Away to Jesus', 'Swing Low, Sweet Chariot' and 'Freedom Train' (and many of the other train songs) referred to the 'Underground Railroad' that helped slaves escape to the North.

It was in 1903 that slave music would be given a name.

One night in 1903, W. C. Handy, a local band-leader, was waiting for a train in Tutwiler, Mississippi, when he was startled by another black man singing.

> His clothes were rags; his feet peeped out of his shoes. His face had on it some of the sadness of the ages. As he played, he pressed a knife on the strings of the guitar in a manner popularised by Hawaiian guitarists who used steel strings. The effect was unforgettable. His songs too, struck me instantly. The singer repeated the line three times, accompanying himself on the guitar with the weirdest music I had ever heard.

That strange music played by the mysterious, unknown musician was the blues, although no one yet knew it by that name.

George W. Johnson recorded the first blues, 'Laughing Song', in 1895, while W. C. Handy's composition 'Memphis Blues' in 1912 was the first to include 'blues' in a song title. Eight years later, Mamie Smith was the first black female to record a blues vocal on 'Crazy Blues'.

Originally called 'race music', it was known mainly within the poor black communities, but many artists playing blues and jazz found fame, including Leadbelly, Bessie Smith, Louis Armstrong, Duke Ellington and Billie Holliday.

Sun Studios in Memphis was the only place where black musicians could record in the South and its owner, Sam Phillips, was convinced that he would make a fortune if he could find a white artist who could recreate this music. When Elvis Presley walked into the studio, Phillips found his man. Elvis was the gateway for rhythm and blues to enter mainstream America, and beyond. Through his impact on the Beatles, the Rolling Stones, Bob Dylan, Bruce Springsteen, U2, and countless others, the blues changed the musical landscape for ever, and ensured that American popular music became the most influential in the world.

Conclusion

Africa still bears the scars that slavery cut into her land.

Africa now is the only continent where poverty is rising, life expectancy is falling and global trade has dropped by two thirds in the past 25 years.

From the past, the ghosts of slavetimes reach out and touch us today, marking prejudicial thoughts for the way things are. We are quick to blame weather, drought, God, floods, natural disasters, inept and indifferent NGOs, corrupt leaders, institutional corruption, religion, politicians, dictators, gigabyte corporations, greed, bad decisions and so on for the state of our world, and frequently the past plays out a role in our present.

We live in a media age where things rise and fade in a dizzyingly fast-moving agenda. Modern campaigns such as Make Poverty History focus on strategic priorities, and we are becoming aware that real change belongs with justice alongside charity.

There are issues to address, but no one should shrink from their past. It is our personal and collective history, when faced, that will enrich our life, enhance our character and create a culture for change.

Until we learn from the past, we will never truly understand the present, or be able to deal with the future.

American tombstone

These bitter words were carved on a tomb in Concord, Massachusetts:

> God wills us free
> Man wills us slaves.
> I will as God wills,
> God's will be done.

Here lies the body of John Jack, a native of Africa, who died March, 1773, aged about sixty years.

Though born in a land of slavery, he was born free. Though he lived in a land of liberty, he lived a slave.

Though not long before death, the grand tyrant gave him his final emancipation, and set him on a footing with kings . . .

Bibliography

In this chapter on 'The transatlantic slave trade and how it ended' I have drawn from several excellent sources and I wish to acknowledge them here with thanks.

Kevin Bales, *Understanding Global Slavery* (University of California Press, 2005).

Ottobah Cugoana, *Thoughts on the Evil of Slavery* (Penguin Classics).

Gale Cameron and Stan Crooke, *Liverpool – Capital of the Slave Trade* (Birkenhead Press, 1992).

Frederick Douglass, *Classic Slave Narratives* (Signet Classics, 2002).

Olaudah Equiano, *Classic Slave Narratives* (Signet Classics, 2002).

Susanne Everett, *History of Slavery* (Bison, 1978).

Adam Hochschild, *Bury the Chains* (Pan Books, 2005).

Harriet Jacobs, *Incidents in the Life of a Slave Girl* (Dover, 2001).

Mike Kaye, *Over 200 Years of Campaigning against Slavery* (Anti-Slavery International, 2005).

Henry Marsh, *Slavery and Race* (David & Charles, 1974).

S. I. Martin, *Britain's Slave Trade* (Channel Four Books, 1999).

Mike Morris, *Slave Trade* (Peaceworks, 1999).

Rosemary Rees, *Britain and the Slave Trade* (Heinemann, 1995)

Rosemarie Robotham (ed.), *Spirits of the Passage* (Simon & Schuster, 1997).

John Simkin, *Slavery, Black History* (Spartacus Educational, 1988).

Hugh Thomas, *The Slave Trade* (Picador, 1997).

Anthony Tibbles (ed.), *Transatlantic Slavery* (National Museums Liverpool, 2005).

James Walvin, *Atlas of Slavery* (Pearson Longman, 2006).

Other publications that were also useful include:

Roger Anstey and P. E. H. Hair, *Liverpool, the African Slave Trade and Abolition* (1976).

Kevin Bales, *Disposable People* (University of California Press, 1999).

David Davis, *Inhuman Bondage* (Oxford University Press, 2006).

Robert Dawson, *British Gypsy Slavery* (Robert Dawson, 2001).

Alan Gallay, *The Indian Slave Trade* (Yale University Press, 2002).

Neil Grant, *The Savage Trade* (Kestrel Books, 1980).

Harry Kelsey, *Queen Elizabeth's Slave Trader* (Yale University Press, 2003).

Daniel Mannix and Malcolm Cowley, *Black Cargoes* (Penguin Books, 1962).

Edmund Morgan, *American Slavery, American Freedom* (Norton, 2003).

Charlotte and Denis Plimmer, *Slavery the Anglo-American Involvement* (Barnes and Noble Books, 1973).

James Pope-Hennessy, *Sins of the Fathers* (Weidenfeld and Nicholson, 1968).

Simon Schama, *Rough Crossings* (BBC Books, 2005).

Ronald Segal, *Islam's Black Slaves* (Atlantic Books, 2001).

James Walvin, *Black Ivory* (Harper Collins, 1992).

Steven Wise, *Though the Heavens May Fall* (Pimlico, 2006).

See also:
www.setallfree.net
www.stopthetraffik.org
www.brycchancarey.com
www.spartacus.schoolnet.co.uk/slavery.htm
www.antislavery.org

DANNY SMITH

Danny Smith lives in Surrey with his wife Joan and their three children, Jessica, Rachel and Luke. An Anglo-Indian, he has published widely on rock music and human rights. He is the co-founder, with David Alton, of Jubilee Campaign, a human rights pressure group with consultative status at the UN, and of the international human rights charity Jubilee Action.

For more information, visit the websites at www.jubileecampaign.co.uk and www.jubileeaction.co.uk, or e-mail Danny direct at danny@jubileecampaign.co.uk.

12: African abolitionists and their struggle for freedom

Tony Warner, Black History Walks

A long history

The black presence in England dates back at least 2,000 years to the Roman invasion of Britain. Africans in Rome and subjects of the North African colonies were present at every level of society, as evidenced by the Libyan-born Emperor Septimus Severus, who died in York in AD 211.

More than 1,000 years later there was clearly a black presence in London, as in 1601 Queen Elizabeth I made her famous proclamation that she was 'highly discontented to understand the great numbers of negars and Blackamores which are crept into this realm . . . who are fostered and relieved here to the great annoyance of her own liege people'. She called for their immediate deportation, which she had already asked for in 1596. This racist attitude towards black people living in Britain would echo down the centuries.

Her edict did not work, however, because in 1731 the Lord Mayor of London banned black people from taking up any trade, a policy that forced people into poverty.

Anti-slavery activists

Ukawsaw Gronniosaw was a prince from the borders of Chad/ Nigeria. He was sold into bondage, but later became a soldier who served in Cuba and Martinique. The British army had a habit of 'recruiting' as well as buying slaves; such soldiers were then used to suppress the numerous plantation revolts *and* fight against other Africans and Indians in the wars which expanded the Empire.

Ukawsaw lived in Petticoat Lane, London and published his slave narrative in 1772. It was the first of what would become a genre of literature, which would play a major part in informing the public of what life was like for enslaved people. This form of resistance was vital to counteract the pro-slavery propaganda.

That year also saw the Mansfield decision and his estimate that there were 15,000 black people in England. That number would have increased somewhat with the arrival of the Black Loyalists in the 1780s. Loyalists were African-Americans who had fought for their freedom, and Britain, in the American War of Independence.

In 1773 Phyllis Wheatley, originally of West Africa, lived in the Tower Hamlets area. Her book *Poems on Various Subjects: Religious and Moral* was the first published by an African woman (at least in the post-slavery era, as there were many female scholars in the ancient African civilisations). Her ability to read, write and express herself astonished those with racist views and helped make the case for African humanity.

In the same year, Ignatius Sancho ran a grocery shop in Charles Street, London W1. He wrote poetry, and a series of letters, the posthumous sale of which achieved a huge readership and helped sway public opinion. He records being abused for the colour of his skin when out with his family – an experience which is still common today.

Olaudah Equiano is one of the most famous African-British abolitionists. Kidnapped as a boy in Nigeria, he was forced into slavery, bought his freedom, served in the Royal Navy and voyaged to the Arctic. Sometime resident of 53 Baldwin Gardens, London EC1, Olaudah published his *Interesting Narrative* in 1789 and toured the country giving abolitionist speeches. He was personally involved in campaigning against the *Zong* massacre.

Olaudah was not alone in his anti-slavery struggles. In 1789 he co-signed a letter published in the *Diary* newspaper. The letter condemned slavery and those who defended it. The 'Sons of Africa', as they were known, included Joseph Sanders, Bough Gegansmel, Cojoh Ammere, Thomas Cooper, William Green, George Robert Mandeville, Bernard Elliot Griffiths and Ottobah Cugoana.

John Marrant was born free in New York in 1755. He became an accomplished musician, but was press-ganged into the Royal Navy during the American War of Independence. He later became a Methodist minister and went to Nova Scotia, where many other black loyalists had been dumped. He returned to England and in 1790 published *A Journal of the Rev John Marrant from 1785–1790*. At the time it was the most detailed account of black community life and missionary work ever published.

William Davidson was a Jamaican radical who fought for equality. In 1820 he resolved to assassinate cabinet members while they were dining in Grosvenor Square. For his efforts in what was known as the 'Cato Street conspiracy', he was first hanged and then beheaded at Newgate Gaol (where the Old Bailey now stands). The conspiracy had been infiltrated by an agent provocateur, who encouraged them to take extreme action and then informed the authorities.

Also involved in fighting for equal rights was Bill Richmond, a black man who in 1806 owned his own gym in Trafalgar Square and coached Lord Byron, among others. He grew up in Northumberland and developed his boxing skills after repeatedly being insulted about his colour. After several such fights, his reputation allowed him to move up the ranks. As a skilled cabinetmaker he could little afford to damage his hands, but nevertheless he took on the awesome Tom Cribb in a prize fight in 1805. He lost, but the profits guaranteed him independence.

SLAVERY NOW – AND THEN

Henry Beckford was an emancipated slave and abolitionist. He was one of the many black men who attended debates in parliament. He features with two other black men in the famous Benjamin Robert Haydon painting *The Anti Slavery Society Convention of 1840* in the National Portrait Gallery.

Frederick Douglas, the leader of black America, spent two years in London. His autobiography, published in 1845, revealed his location to the slave master from whom he had escaped. Fearing recapture, he sought refuge in London for two years. While he was there, his British friends collected money and 'bought' him from his ex-master. He was then able to return to America as a free man, but not before he delivered anti-slavery speeches in places like Leeds and Taunton. Douglas later became the first US ambassador to Haiti in 1891.

The true story

The fact that most of this information is unknown and indeed sometimes disbelieved by the general public illustrates how effective the education system, both formal and informal, has been in portraying a false version of history. This version promotes an ideology where black people were passive victims in the fight against slavery and its monster child racism. Indeed, the very idea that Wilberforce and white English liberals brought freedom to the grateful Africans is another manifestation of a white supremacist thought process.

The real story is that African people resisted and fought for equality using any means necessary, be it fists (Bill Richmond), books (Ukawsaw Gronniosaw), speeches (Olaudah Equiano), or by massive and violent uprisings (Haitian Revolution, 1791; Sam Sharpe Rebellion of Jamaica, 1831).

The racism which justified the slave trade and the Empire has become endemic and normalised, to the extent that it underlies the very culture in which we live. The struggle continues against new manifestations of racism, be it stop-and-search, school exclusions, immigration controls, racist murders or deaths in custody.

The continued ignorance and collective amnesia of the true history of this country help to create an environment in which slavery continues to this day in England and around the world.

TONY WARNER

Tony Warner is a management consultant specialising in anti-racist practice and diversity. He has used history to enliven training courses and runs monthly educational events throughout London. He also manages African history walking tours in the City of London and the West End. He can be contacted on blackhistorywalks@hotmail.co.uk.

13: William Wilberforce: A profile

Steve Chalke MBE, Oasis Trust,
Stop The Traffik

Steve Chalke recalls the life of William Wilberforce, a man of profound con-
viction who fought against the prevailing orthodoxy of his time . . .

Late on the evening of the 26th July 1833, the elderly Wilberforce
was brought the long-awaited news that the bill to abolish slavery
had finally passed its third reading in the House of Commons. As
its passage through the House of Lords was not in doubt, to all
intents the emancipation of slaves was at last a reality. Three days
later, at the age of 74, 'Wilber', as he was known by family and
friends, the champion of slaves, was dead.

Wilberforce's great goal

'God Almighty has set before me two great objects,' wrote
Wilberforce some 46 years earlier, in his diary for the 28th
October 1787, 'the suppression of the Slave Trade and the
Reformation of Manners.' His goal was much wider than ending
slavery and he engaged in issues as diverse as penal reform, popular education, factory legislation, colonial policy, parliamentary
reform, animal rights and many more. But he soon came to

believe that it was slavery that was the most damning symptom of the nation's moral malaise.

Late in the eighteenth century, tens of thousands of Africans were still being torn from their homes and families, and transported in appalling conditions across the Atlantic Ocean, mostly to the West Indies, to be sold as slaves. And although an end to this barbarous practice was supported by a growing number of leading Europeans, such a move faced fierce opposition from the merchants, whom it had made very wealthy and powerful. The abolitionists needed a champion to fight their cause: a champion with enormous energy, commitment, political skill and good connections. As a leader from a different age, Kenneth Kaunda, was later to point out, 'What a country needs more than anything else is not a Christian ruler in the palace but a Christian prophet within earshot.' For his generation, Wilberforce was that man.

The 'cloud of witnesses'

In an age when we have come to idolise independence, to view self-reliance as life's ultimate goal, and to require of our heroes an impossible omni-competence, we do well to heed the words of John Pollock. 'Wilberforce proves', he wrote, 'that one man can change his times, but he cannot do it alone.'

For all his strengths, Wilberforce equally had his weaknesses. His health was never good, he was often hesitant, overly cautious, shy and filled with self-doubt. He could be muddled and disorganised, to the extent that even his faithful friend William Pitt would never grant him the cabinet position for which he always longed. So what of the 'cloud of witnesses', who surrounded Wilberforce and kept him racing?

John Wesley was always more than a preacher. He was a passionate prophet of social reform, and Wilberforce owed a huge amount to his influence and example. In 1774 Wesley had written *Thoughts on Slavery*, one of the first pamphlets against the slave trade, and in 1791, aged 87, the day before the onset of his brief final illness, he wrote to Wilberforce to encourage him: 'Unless God has raised you up for this very thing, you will be worn out by the opposition of men and devils. But if God be for you, who can be against you . . .'

In October 1784, Wilberforce set out on holiday. Before leaving, he met Isaac Milner, whom he had known as a boy and who was now a clergyman and tutor at Queen's College, Cambridge. William was impressed by Milner as 'very much a man of the world' and 'lively and dashing in his conversation'. On impulse, he invited him to join the trip. Wilberforce, like most of his contemporaries in high places, gave formal assent to the doctrines of the Church of England, and was a regular churchgoer. However, during the long holiday, the two men read widely and debated, and as a result Wilberforce concluded that 'in the true sense of the word I was not a Christian'.

He so enjoyed Milner's company that the following summer they set off again, this time for Austria. By the third week of October, what Wilberforce was later to call his 'great change' had taken place. Serving God was his new life goal – but as a result he now longed to escape from the clamour of politics and public life, and find peaceful life in solitude.

Wilberforce encountered John Newton as a boy and was enthralled by the sermons of this jolly ex-sea captain, ex-lecher and ex-slave trader turned Methodist preacher and hymnwriter. Now torn between following Christ and his career in politics, it was the advice of the ageing Newton that he sought out on the 7th December 1785. He had already written to William Pitt, by then prime minister, to explain that if he was going to live for God, he must withdraw from the world of politics – a view held by most evangelicals at this time. Try as he might, Pitt had been unable to change Wilberforce's mind, and it was only after Wilberforce had made the visit to see his old boyhood hero that the matter was resolved.

Two years later, Newton wrote to Wilberforce with words which must echo what had been said on that day. 'It is hoped and believed that the Lord has raised you up for the good of his Church and the good of the nation.'

STEVE CHALKE

In 1985 Steve Chalke set up the Oasis Trust in order to open a hostel for homeless young people. Oasis now has over 400 staff, students and volunteers, pioneering educational, health-care and housing initiatives in the UK and across the globe. For more information, visit www.oasistrust.org.

In 2006 Steve became chair of the Stop The Traffik steering group. Stop The Traffik is a global coalition campaigning against people trafficking, through preventing the sale of people, prosecuting the traffickers and protecting the victims. To find out more, visit www.stopthetraffik.org.

Conclusion: Scars on the soul of Africa

Professor The Lord Alton of Liverpool

David Alton reflects on the roots of a trade as old as mankind and the wounds it has left on both British and African history . . .

A gathering organised by former President Mathieu Kerekou of Benin brought together Africans, Europeans and Americans. No one who went to it could come away unaffected. The enormity of what happened in West Africa in past centuries poses a whole range of questions for today.

The challenge for Africa is summed up by President Kerekou's own story.

Baptised a Catholic, he became a Marxist and eventually the military leader of this West African state. Tucked away between Togo, Burkino Faso, Niger and its huge neighbour Nigeria, this former French colony has a population of about six million people. In 1990, Kerekou called free elections. He lost the election and handed over power to his opponents. It was the first time in Africa that a peaceful democratic transition had occurred in a free election. In 1995 Kerekou received his reward and was voted back into office. He has appointed several evangelical Christians to advisory and ministerial posts, and speaks openly of the importance of his religious belief.

Benin is the birthplace of the voodoo practice. It is the country's official religion and is very much in evidence. Sixty-five per cent of the country's people are said to be of traditional religions; 15 per cent are Muslim and 20 per cent are Christian.

While on a visit to the US, Kerekou made a speech describing his own antecedents. He said that his forebears were black slave traders, capturing and selling other Africans to the white slave traders. Many of the black American delegates said that this was the most shocking part of their own history and the part which they found most difficult to confront. 'How could a black brother sell their brother or their sister to be a slave?' asked Bishop David Perrin. By apologising publicly to the black American diaspora, President Kerekou lanced a festering boil.

Between 1701 and 1810 around 5.7 million people were taken into slavery, 2 million coming from the Slave Coast where Benin is situated. Around 39 per cent went to the Caribbean, 38 per cent to Brazil, 17 per cent to South America and 6 per cent to North America. Many of the slaves were shipped out of Africa from the Bight of Benin to the port of Ouidah, which is situated near Cotonou, the present capital. Not since I visited the Holocaust memorial at Yad Vashem in Israel have I experienced such harrowing emotions. Captured slaves were brought to Ouidah, where the Portuguese had built a fort – which today houses a small museum where many of the artefacts involved in this revolting trade are exhibited. Inside the fort stands the Immaculate Conception, built by the Portuguese.

At the nearby Auction Place under the Whipping Tree, the slaves were sold to European traders. From here they had to walk the slave route to the shores of the Atlantic. I followed in their footsteps to a staging post called the Zomai (which means 'where the light is not allowed to go'). From here, according to ritual, the slaves would be taken to the Tree of Forgetfulness. Men would be made to walk around it nine times, women seven times. It was believed that this would strip them of their memory – that they would lose their identity, forget their origins, their families and their countries. Slavery is debasing in itself. This forced 'amnesia' was the final assault on a person's humanity.

At Zomai, sick, disabled or elderly people were picked out and thrown into a common grave. Some were buried alive. Today the memorial of Zoungbodji marks this place of holocaust. Here we removed our shoes, stood in silence as candles flickered in a gentle breeze, and silently wondered what atonement would put right such inhumanity.

The slaves to be deported would then be taken to the Tree of Return. Here they had to turn three times in the hope that, although their bodies would never stand on these shores again, one day their spirit would return. Then they were finally on the road to the Door of No Return, marked today by an archway, through which men, women and children would pass before boarding a boat waiting for the 'Middle Passage' of this evil triangular trade plied between Europe, Africa and the Americas.

Before leaving the Door of No Return, some of the delegates from the conference started to sing the hymn 'Amazing Grace'. I wondered whether they knew that this hymn had been written by the English former slave captain John Newton. When he renounced the trade, his evidence helped the abolitionist cause, led by the Christian campaigner William Wilberforce.

If there are unresolved questions for the sellers of slaves, there remain questions, too, for the buyers and the victims.

The trade before 1730 was dominated by London, but was overtaken by Bristol in the 1730s, only to be eclipsed by Liverpool in the 1750s. In 1797, one in four ships leaving Liverpool was a slaver. Liverpool agents handled five eighths of the slave trade in Europe. In his *Journal of a Slave Trader* John Newton wrote, 'I have no sufficient data to warrant calculation but I suppose not less than one hundred thousand slaves are annually exported from all parts of Africa and that more than one half these are exported in English ships.' The Liverpool historian Ramsey Muir estimated that in

1807 a staggering £17 million was generated in Liverpool through the slave trade. This was the darkest chapter in the city's history.

What struck me about the Benin conference was the willingness of the people who had suffered so much at the hands of the others to recognise that it was time to clean the slate and to forgive. The victims of the slave trade have every right to feel anger and bitterness. Who could blame them for becoming prisoners of their history? One delegate put it well when he said, 'We sometimes forget that the white people today are not the same people who pursued the slave trade. They are the whites of yesterday, not of today.'

I vividly recall the young black woman who said to me at the time of the Toxteth riots of Liverpool in 1981, 'Since the slave trade 200 years ago, we have simply moved half a mile up the road.' In other words, much of the social injustice, racism and prejudice on which the slave trade was built continues to manifest itself in the ill-treatment of minorities today. The consequences of the slave trade and the continuation of the principles of slavery, through the contemporary trafficking of human beings, remain urgent issues for today.

The bicentenary of 2007 gives us the opportunity to tell the story of how a group of men and women – black and white – exerted great moral and practical pressure to bring about change. It also provides us with the opportunity to focus on contemporary forms of slavery – massive exploitation of labour, the caste-based atrocities against groups like the Indian Dalits, human trafficking, and, in countries like the Sudan and Niger, the continuation of practices which would have been recognised by Wilberforce and Equiano.

In remembering the infamies of the slave trade, we should also remember those black and white people who saw it for what it was, refused to collaborate and denounced it.

In the British parliament the young William Wilberforce led the abolitionist cause. He spent 40 long years fighting huge vested interests.

In 1782, on introducing a Bill for Abolition, Wilberforce began his speech with this cry from the heart: 'Africa, Africa, your sufferings have been the theme that has arrested and engages a heart. Your suffering no tongue can express, no language impart.' How apposite those words remain as we consider the continuing depredations in Darfur and the Congo. If you take Sudan, Congo, Rwanda and Uganda together, some seven million people have been killed in the past 15 years. This is Africa's Great War, but it hardly rates a paragraph in the papers. In 1807 Wilberforce persuaded parliament to make the slave trade illegal – against fierce opposition from the profiteers of slavery. In 1833, as Wilberforce was dying, the news was brought to him that the British parliament had finally abolished slavery throughout all its territories.

Slavery is not a historic phenomenon. We must learn from the past, but not dwell in it. Men like Wilberforce and Equiano fundamentally changed attitudes and laws, but their example will count for little unless we put the same ideals into practice in our own times. Their stories remind us that when small stones move, landslides can happen.

PROFESSOR THE LORD ALTON OF LIVERPOOL

For 25 years David Alton served as a city councillor or MP in Liverpool. Today he sits as an independent cross-bench peer in the House of Lords. He was the country's youngest city councillor, the youngest member of the House of Commons and then the youngest life peer. In 1992 he announced that he would not stand again as a Liberal Democrat after the party made support for abortion a party policy for the first time. Earlier in the day, at the same conference, an animal welfare motion had passed which included protection for goldfish on sale in amusement arcades and funfairs.

On behalf of Liverpool John Moores University, where he is Professor of Citizenship, he has staged the Roscoe Lectures on Citizenship and created a good citizens awards scheme that is operating in 900 schools in the north-west of England.

Lord Alton is co-founder of the Jubilee Campaign, a national patron of LIFE, and a member of the bioethics committee appointed by the Catholic Bishops of England and Wales. He is the author of eleven books and a Visiting Fellow of St Andrew's University.

Further details about Lord Alton, including his articles, can be found at www.davidalton.com.

PART THREE: TAKE ACTION

Be inspired. Get involved. Pray. Act. Give.

We can and must play our part in fighting the twenty-first-century evil of modern slavery. Here are the websites and contact details for people and organisations linked with this book.

Take action

Be inspired. Get involved. Pray. Act. Give.

Just Right magazine

Write for a free copy and a special edition on 'Modern Slavery' featuring many of the authors in this book. This magazine will keep you informed on important human rights issues and show action you can take. *Just Right* is edited by Danny Smith.
info@justright.org.uk
Just Right, 96 High Street, Guildford, Surrey, GU1 3HE

David Alton
www.davidalton.co.uk

Anti-Slavery International
Thomas Clarkson House
The Stableyard
Broomgrove Road
London SW9 9TL
United Kingdom
www.antislavery.org

Black History Walks
blackhistorywalks@hotmail.co.uk

Christian Solidarity Worldwide
PO Box 99
New Malden
Surrey KT3 3YF
United Kingdom
www.csw.org.uk

Dalit Freedom Network
5350 S Roslyn Ste 200
Greenwood Village CO 80111-2123
USA
www.dalitnetwork.org

DFN's partner organisation for child sponsorship:
Operation Mobilisation UK
FREEPOST
Oswestry
Shropshire SY10 7BR
United Kingdom

ECPAT UK
Grosvenor Gardens House
35–37 Grosvenor Gardens
London SW1W 0BS
United Kingdom
www.ecpat.org.uk

The Evangelical Alliance
186 Kennington Park Road
London SE11 4BT
United Kingdom
www.eauk.org

Free the Slaves
1012 14th Street
NW Ste 600
Washington DC 20005
USA
www.freetheslaves.net

Humanitarian Aid Relief Trust (HART)
3 Arnellan House
146 Slough Lane
Kingsbury
London NW9 8XJ
United Kingdom
www.hart-uk.org

Jubilee Action
96 High Street
Guildford
Surry GU1 3HE
United Kingdom
www.jubileeaction.co.uk

Jubilee Campaign
96 High Street
Guildford
Surrey GU1 3HE
United Kingdom
www.jubileecampaign.co.uk

Jubilee Campaign USA
9689-C Main Street
Fairfax, VA 22031
USA
www.jubileecampaign.org

Just Law International
9689-C Main Street
Fairfax
Virginia 22031
USA
www.justlawintl.com

Peaceworks
www.peaceworks.org.uk

Preda Foundation Inc.
Upper Kalaklan
Olongapo City 2200
Philippines
www.preda.org
www.preda.net

Anita Roddick
www.anitaroddick.com
www.takeitpersonally.com

Ben Rogers
www.benrogers.org.uk

Set All Free
www.setallfree.net

Stop the Traffik
115 Southwark Bridge Road
London SE1 0AX
United Kingdom
www.stopthetraffic.org

Stop the Traffik has been launched by the *Oasis Trust*:
www.oasistrust.org

Hazel Thompson
www.hazelthompson.com

True Vision
Order Kate Blewett's and Brian Woods' award-winning documentary *Slavery* – and other outstanding films: www.truevisiontv.com

True Vision's powerful documentary *Slavery*, exposing slavery on the cocoa plantations of West Africa, led to the first ever anti-slavery protocol introduced by the industry. This was signed between major chocolate manufacturers, NGOs such as Free the Slaves, and other major parties with the intention of eliminating slavery from the cocoa supply chain.

Anti-Slavery International recommend the following:

(1) Contact the major chocolate companies
Tell them that you support policies that end the use of illegal child labour and forced adult labour on farms supplying cocoa. Ask them to monitor and enforce such policies and publicise results. Also ask the companies to develop contacts with local NGOs and ensure that changes they make are integrated within broader initiatives on trafficking, illegal child labour and forced labour. Contact the four major chocolate companies. Write, fax or e-mail them directly from their website:

Public Affairs
Nestlé S.A. Centre
Avenue Nestlé 55
Case postale 353
CH-1800 Vevey
Switzerland
Fax: +41 21 921 18 85

www.nestle.com
www.nestle.co.uk

Consumer Affairs
Mars Inc.
800 High Street
Hackettstown
NJ 07840
United States
www.mars.com

Consumer Relations Department UK
Cadbury Trebor Bassett
PO Box 12
Bournville
Birmingham
B30 2LU
United Kingdom
Fax: +44 (0) 121 451 4192
www.cadbury.co.uk
www.cadburyschweppes.com

Hershey Foods Corporation
Consumer Relations
100 Crystal A Drive
Hershey
PA 17033-0815
United States
Tel: + 1 800 468 1714
www.hersheygifts.com

(2) Support Fair Trade and buy their products
If your local retailer does not stock Fair Trade products, write and
ask them to!

Support people like Father Shay Cullen and the Preda Foundation,

who help local communities. Check Preda's products and alternative world shops:
ww.preda.net
pretrade@info.com.ph

British Association for Fair Trade Shops is a network of independent fair trade shops across the UK. It was established in 1995 and seeks to promote fair trade retailing in the UK. It is also a member of the Network of European World Shops and is an information, support and campaigning organisation for its members.
www.bafts.org.uk

Seek out companies such as our friends at Clipper Tea and support their products:
www.clipper-teas.com

To find out more, see:

www.fairtrade.net
www.ifat.org
www.fairtrade.org.uk

(3) Keep up to date with developments
Be informed.

(4) Express your concern to your political representatives
Ask them to communicate your message to the relevant authorities.

The following suggestions were taken from People & Planet, a network of student groups working for a just and sustainable world: www.peopleandplanet.org.

Get writing

Letter-writing is an age-old technique within the social change movement. Letter-writing meetings are often a good idea, because even with the best intentions, people don't always get around to writing the letter on their own. There are a few things to remember:

- **Be polite and stick to the point.** It might be frustrating, but you'll get a far more useful reply.
- **Give the person you are lobbying a good reason to listen to you** (your potential vote?).
- **A letter will get more attention than a postcard.** It shows you've put more effort in.
- **Avoid exaggeration** – it does more harm than good.
- **Keep a file of correspondence,** both of your letters and the replies.

Contact Your MP

Your MP can help you by doing the following things.

- **Asking oral questions**: these are tabled two weeks in advance to a government department and are drawn by ballot. There is only time for 10–15 questions to be answered.
- **Asking written questions**: they can ask an unlimited number of written questions, usually to elicit information from a government department. This can be done on your behalf.
- **Writing to a government minister/European commisioner on your behalf.**
- **Signing an Early Day Motion** (a kind of parliamentary petition).

MPs will answer letters from their constituents before any other, as this is their duty. However, in most cases they will forward your letter to the relevant minister, government department or party spokesperson and hence you are likely to get a standard reply.

Often this reply will have little relevance to the original points that you raised, so it is better to ask specific questions and to enquire about your MP's personal opinion. Try spreading letter-writing around the group, with each person addressing only one important point in their letter.

If you don't get the response you want, don't just sit there and take it. Pick up your pen, or put fingers to keyboard, and restate your case, if necessary pointing out the errors in the reply.

Contact details

You can find the address of your MP, MSP, AM or MEP through the following sources:

MPs

Post: House of Commons, London, SW1A 0AA,
or call 020 7219 3000 for their constituency address
Full details: www.parliament.uk/commons/lib/alms.htm
Fax: www.faxyourmp.com

MEPs

Post: European Parliament UK Office, 2 Queen Anne's Gate, London SW1H 9AA,
or call 020 7227 4300 for their constituency address
Full details: www.europarl.org.uk/uk_meps/MembersMain.htm

MSPs

Post: The Scottish Parliament, Edinburgh EH99 1SP,
or call 0131 348 5817 for their constituency address
E-mail: firstname.surname.msp@scottish.parliament.uk
Full details: www.scottish.parliament.uk/msps (click on 'biography')

AMs

Post: National Assembly for Wales, Cardiff Bay, Cardiff CF99 1NA, or call 029 20 825111 for their constituency address
Full details: www.wales.gov.uk/who/constit_e.htm

Wilberforce

by John Pollock

Born in Hull in 1759, William Wilberforce was destined to become one of Britain's most influential statesmen, having been influenced himself by men like Whitefield, Wesley and, most of all, John Newton.

Wilberforce introduced his first anti-slave trade motion in the House of Commons in 1788 with a speech that lasted three-and-a-half-hours, appealing to the dictates of conscience, the principles of justice and the law of God.

The motion was defeated – but Wilberforce continued his campaign until the slave trade was abolished and went on to fight against slavery itself right up to his death. Just as he died on July 29, 1833, Wilberforce was informed that Parliament had finally agreed to the emancipation of slaves.

His fight is faithfully recorded here as one of the most courageous and vital political battles in history.

> 'One of the most moving and memorable historical biographies in our time . . . it should on no account be missed.'
>
> *Church Times*

> 'John Pollock gives a detailed picture of Wilberforce's life and character and includes some important new information.'
>
> *The Observer*

> 'Vivid and painstakingly researched biography.'
>
> *Daily Telegraph*

 **Kingsway**

www.kingway.co.uk